PENGUIN BO

The Terrible

Yrsa Daley-Ward is a writer and poet of mixed West Indian
and West African heritage. Born to a Jamaican mother
and a Nigerian father, Yrsa was raised by her devout
Seventh-Day Adventist grandparents in the small town of
Chorley in the north of England. She lives in New York.

The Terrible

YRSA DALEY-WARD

PENGUIN BOOKS

PENGUIN BOOKS

UK | USA | Canada | Ireland | Australia
India | New Zealand | South Africa

Penguin Books is part of the Penguin Random House group of companies
whose addresses can be found at global.penguinrandomhouse.com.

First published by Penguin Books 2018
003

Set in 11/14 pt Adobe Garamond Pro
Typeset by Jouve (UK), Milton Keynes
Printed and bound in Great Britain by Clays Ltd, Elcograf S.p.A.

A CIP catalogue record for this book is available from the British Library

ISBN: 978-1-846-14982-5

www.greenpenguin.co.uk

For Little Roo.

in love with how it happened so far,
even the terrible things.

and God, there were terrible things.

The Terrible

Prologue

My little brother and I saw a unicorn in the garden in the late nineties. I'm telling you.

Neither one of us made it up; it was as real as anything else. Sometimes, when the world around us grew indistinct, when facts would blur into less certain truths and frightening things looked set to occur, the two of us could see clearly into the Fourth Dimension. So when Linford James was on a ladder at midnight, banging on the bedroom windows, shouting at Mum

and later, when the colour in his throat deepened and they were nose to nose, neither one of them spotted the unicorn. Adults went about their lives missing beauty all the time.

Little Roo was six. I was ten. The unicorn strode a couple of majestic laps of the garden, before vanishing completely into the rosebush. The Fourth Dimension was our only explanation for this. We weren't dreaming.

That night, Mum called the police. The next evening, Linford was sleeping in her bed again, snoring the walls down in his frightening manner.

The unicorn wasn't the only strange thing. Living in Chorley, up in the North, we were closer to the sky than most. What luck. Little Roo often saw things written in the stars. Signs, Facts and Other Things. I'm telling you.

He knew why adults said the things they said. And why they didn't *mean* the things they said
and even less what they did. Sometimes it wasn't answers that he found, but entirely perfect questions.

A genius, my little brother.

Marcia Daley-Ward aka '*mum*'

had a slim waist (in the very beginning),
soft hair
a gorgeous smile (pearly arcs, those teeth. Shining church
doors).
Marcia had smiling eyes
loose hips
could dance as well as anyone on television
lived with her grandparents in Kingston, Jamaica,
and she was oh so kind,
had some art about her.
When told to go into the woods to choose a branch with
which her grandfather would beat her little brother
(for some tiny offence) chose a weak branch that came apart in
her grandfather's hand
and earned a beating too.

Marcia
was fourteen and still skinny when she flew over to England,
alone and terrified
with a baby in her belly. The boyfriend at that time was not
the baby's daddy
but none of that mattered, because everything was about to
change. She had been sent for, finally, by her mother
and would be as far away from all of these men as God
would allow.

She trembled when stepping off the plane. She was about to
see her parents, for the first time in years. How would she tell
them? How would she explain?

Marcia
is sixteen with screaming Baby Samson, in the North West of
England.
What a mess
and he's only getting bigger. A real-life mini-man; the sum
of several fears. Growing and growing, faster than she can
handle. She curses the Lord Above. Marcia's parents step in.
Especially when little Samson rides his small tricycle all the
way to Grandma's just to get away from Marcia and her mood
swings. They raise him like a son;
never mind a grandson. He even calls them *'Mum and Dad'*
leaves Marcia's title
blank.

Alone,
Marcia trains to be a nurse.

So
soon, Marcia, the student nurse, is twenty-six. The man
she loves is a dark, beautiful scholar with some height to him,
some education
and a wife and family in Nigeria. Guinness is his drink.
He'll be the last one to leave the pub. The last one home and,
most every night,

he turns towards her with those irresistible, glazed eyes,
blackshining. So she can't stay angry, even if she tries.
But his other home calls and the academic year ends
and their time will soon be up. He knows and she knows
that he will not stay, but they make a child anyway.

YRSA
she says. Yrsa. I like the sound of that.

ONE

Aa

Read to me! Mummy would say;
and boy, she and I read. We read our lives out. Right from
the very beginning.
Hot, thick worlds with ladybirds and puffins on their spines.
Watery, cool-mountainous wholewideworlds.
Why didn't anyone help the Little Red Hen make food?
or
Why was the cat so naughty?

And Mummy would point at the picture of the cat who
wouldn't behave. The angry, frowning cat
sitting, arms folded, in the corner.
It's because he needs love, she would say. It's only because
he's frightened.

Why did the lion scream, 'Over my dead body!'
when someone tried to give away his comb? Why did
he bellow,
frightening the entire jungle?

It's because he needs things, she would say,
the lion is lonely and vain.
Mummy was soft. Warm-milk soft
and everything written in our paperworlds
made hot, small sense.

Bb

She lifts me up onto the kitchen counter.

The child is so, so gifted.

She's reading already?

Well, hear for yourself.

And way before school?

Yes, quite. Kids can do anything, you know. It's all in teaching them early. Just look and see how easily she forms the words.

She smiles at me. Her eyes, like honey. Bronzeshining.

You're my *supernova*,
says she.
My thrilling, bright explosion.

Marcia is thirty,
loves Linford
but feels bereft of something. A friend (Sonny, his name)
stays overnight (again) and when her little girl comes to the
door, she ushers her out, quickly.
'Go back to bed.' says she, 'See you in the morning,
baby-girl.
I love you.'
Then she lays back, a hand on her stomach, wondering what
time it will be this dark morning when Sonny the Friend will
make his excuses and disappear off into the town.
Somewhere inside her, Little Roo is beginning
and nobody knows yet but God.

a red home

We moved house. Linford is Mum's boyfriend and we are staying at his place right now. It is a two-up two-down in Warrington. Linford's house is under construction, but getting there. At first it is exciting, moving to this half-built red-brick house with red, red floors. An almost-house. A house nearly on the corner of the street.

The kitchen floor tiles bother me because they are all scratched and uneven and I think there might be germs there.

I have a baby brother these days. I call him Little Roo because he is what older people call *hyperactive* and likes to skip hop around, kangaroo style. Linford is a travelling salesman and sometimes he has to go away for two to three days while Mum is still working nights at the hospital, so we have this babysitter called Bev. Bev the Babysitter smells of parma violets and has yellow wavy hair and long nails and lots of freckles, and talks a lot on the phone late at night. When I'm in bed I can hear her cackling up through the flooring.

My big brother Samson is away, fighting in the army. I miss him holding my hand and walking to school with me. I love my little brother, but he's too small to know how to do things and he cries a lot.

Samson had to get away, he said. He is sorry to leave. But he can't *stand that guy Linford*

and he *had to get away*. Mum tells all this to Bev the Babysitter while they are drinking tea in the morning and Bev tuts and sucks on a cigarette and calls him a 'typical teenager',

'How old is he? Seventeen, eighteen? They're all rotten at that age,' she says

and Mum, still in her blue and white nurse's uniform, looks down at her tea and says, quietly,

'He isn't rotten; they just don't see eye to eye.' And Bev shakes her head and says,

'The army isn't the thing, though, is it? Just teaches them to be violent, I think. Ruins 'em more, I say,'

and Mum gives Bev twenty-five pounds and slowly gets to her feet, holding her head,

and says,

'Well, Beverly, I'd better be getting to bed. Thank you.'

and Beverly nods and puts on her coat.

I am only seven years old and already getting round in the wrong places. The swellings of my little breasts are showing through my clothes, growing into small protruding points

. . . so very fast, says Mum, getting nervous. She works night after night at the local hospital

and frets

and tells me to wear big T-shirts over my nighties – especially the long silky blue one, which is so low cut that it needs three safety pins.

Remember, Linford is not your dad, she says. Wear my orange gown at all times at night now. The one with the flowers. Be mindful.

What is *mindful*?

It means, use your head. You're growing into something else now. All little girls grow and change

and . . .

look,

it is what it is.

It's true. I feel like something new. Something
uncomfortable. Aware of my largeness for my age, the things I
have growing on my front and the one who is *called* Dad
                                                  but is *not* Dad.
Dad is something that I didn't know that I had. Or needed.

Who *is* my dad, then? I ask one day.
He's Nigerian. He's from NIGERIA,
Mum states proudly, as though that answers the question.
Handsome as anything and he's AMAZING. I still love him.
I do.
And he is a PRINCE, you know. Royalty. You have royal
blood in you, you know. We write to each other, you know.
Do you want to see what he looks like?
    I do.
    Mum gets out a photograph from a large envelope marked
'taxes' in the bedside drawer. The Amazing Nigerian has a
round smiling face and smooth dark skin. (Much darker than
Linford and my grandparents.) He is wearing a square cap and
a gown. Mum says it is his graduation outfit. Says he is the
smartest man she knows.

The One, she says, looking off into the distance. God, and you look just like him, you know?

I don't.
He's a grown-up. He's a stranger.
He's some man in a cap and gown.

Some 'facts' are lies; that's the truth of it.
I still have to call Linford 'Dad,'
but my real dad is a university lecturer in Nigeria, who reads
lots of books. Mum says that I am an *African*, which sounds
pretty good. But Granddad says *Africans* are wicked
and sold us into slavery.
Samson is gone. Gone fighting, but for a good reason.
Soldiers die sometimes
but it won't happen to Samson, because we say our prayers at
bedtime.

There might be an *issue* with Linford, Mum says.
What is an *issue*?
An issue is a thing. It's not that he's not Good,
it's just that he has no patience. It's just that he growls a lot.
The lion is quite lonely;
the cat, he just feels bad.
He needs love and is frightened, and we must understand.

Love is a string: Mum loves me and Little Roo. Marcia loves
Linford. I don't know who Linford loves. Marcia says she has
a lovely little girl, with a smile and eyes that are going to break

the men apart. Marcia thinks her child will be a beautiful
thing. Just like your dad, she says.
I loved him.
But he has a wife
and *responsibilities.*
Mum tells me my African name.
Dankyes,
she says
Dankyes Mikuk.
Dankyes means,
'At last! An end to terrible things.'

The blue nightdress is coming apart. I wear the orange robe
as I've been instructed, but one day, Mum says that I am
moving out. She and Little Roo are staying at Linford's
but I have to go. I have to Be Somewhere Else for a While. It's
better that way. I am going to live miles away at Grandma and
Granddad's, where I will have to eat a lot of rice and peas and
go to bed early and go to church all the time and everyone else
will get to stay in Warrington, eating KFC and having fun.
It's only four years, she says. Till Big School. And four years
travels fast.
Marcia says,
'I need to work nights and I need not to worry.'
Mum says it'll just be a matter of four small years
over at Grandma's. Marcia says,
'It'll be over before you know it, little one.'

There is something starting to go wrong. I don't know what
it is. Only that, according to Marcia, my nightdress is a wrong
thing. Dark blue satin. A long, wrong thing. And the red
house is dangerous
   or
I am dangerous
or we are dangerous at the same time,
we are dangerous to each other.
My body is too big to stay home.

Body as trap,
body as trapdoor to a haunted unreal place.

Linford as almost-bad-thing
   but not quite. Linford is a Halfling sometimes frightening
sometimes fun sometimes he takes us for ice cream sometimes he roars
when we don't eat all of our mountains of rice and chicken/ fish/ dead
animal and moats and rivers of gravy and stew – dinner can be an entire
kingdom. Sometimes he shouts, I will smack you people, eat de food NOW
or yuh gonna know about it! And he leaves us in the kitchen with the
horrible red floor with the scratches and countrysides of potato and yam.
Sometimes he gives us fifty-pence pieces that shine and sometimes he buys
us cream soda for the ice cream and we make floats;
   sometimes he does this,
   sometimes he does that.

the grand chapter / the seventh day / the meaning of life

Grandma and Granddad are devout Seventh-Day Adventists. They love Jesus and God, who are actually nearly the same person and all-seeing and powerful and form a trinity with the Holy Spirit.

Nothing is more important than Jesus and God and the Holy Spirit. Anyone who does not know that will be destroyed, thus sayeth the Bible. Anyone who does not know that will go straight to hell, where there will be wailing and pain and disaster.

In this house, we serve God, Jesus and the Holy Spirit. We do not eat shellfish and we do not eat swine, in any of its cunning disguises. (The pig is an unclean meat.) We do not drink Coca-Cola or tea or coffee (because of caffeine, which is DRUGS) or say 'bless you' when someone sneezes, because that is blasphemous and exactly like taking the Lord's name in vain.

There is no jewellery to be worn. We do not adorn ourselves. (Pride.)
If you are black,
i.e. not blessed with Good Long Hair, you can get a wig or a perm – they're necessary, thus allowed. (Acceptable Pride.)

We know all of the Bible, from Genesis to Revelation, and we go to church all day every single Saturday, from sun-up till sunset. Saturday is the seventh day but the people in this country who are definitely not Christians lie and make us think it's Sunday. We are the only true keepers of the Sabbath and everyone else going to church on Sunday is committing a sin and is more than likely going to hell. (Jewish people go to church on Saturdays too but they are sinners in lots of other ways and also they killed Jesus.)

Grandma and Granddad have been in the country for years, retaining their Jamaican customs, ideals and accents. They call each other Mummy and Daddy. Their house is organized and floral with decorative upholstery,

lace tablecloths

net curtains

plastic-coated pictures of Jesus

glass spheres with marble-like patterns in them

plaques inscribed with Bible verses

decorative plates

artificial flowers

and china figurines of beautiful white ladies in gowns with cups of tea

all of which are displayed in glass cases,

a free-standing one in the dining room and a smaller one in the 'front room' which is off limits, for the 'front room' is where the pastor might sit, or sales people, or the insurance man. Important people.

There you might find the bookcase, the expensive floral sofa, the illustrated children's Bible, the gramophone (although it hasn't worked for years), framed photographs of my aunties/ uncles/cousins when they were young, the Good Plates and Good Glasses (painted with brightly coloured birds and flowers. Reserved for Christmas Day, or for Church People who come to dinner).

The back room is our living room, where we eat, sit and watch television. We eat out of yellow bowls and off blue and white willow-patterned crockery. Above our dinner table is a

large painted impression of Christ and the Last Supper, next to
a tall golden clock. God is always watching. Always.

He is *the silent listener to every conversation*, says Grandma,
which is why we have a calendar telling us the exact time of
sunset each Friday, when the Sabbath begins, and why we are
always on our knees, praying. We don't want to burn in hell
on Judgement day with the Pagans, non-believing fools and
other evildoers.

Grandma likes to Look Good Always. She says, 'there's no
excuse for going out 'pon road any old way', and, 'don't look
like nobody don't own you'. (Good and Decent Pride.)

She has beautiful dresses and suits and lots of them are
shiny. She wears perfume from Avon and high-heeled court
shoes to match all of her church hats and handbags, she has
lots of handbags. She is short and round, always cleaning the
house to perfection. Grandma is the best cook that everyone
knows; her rice and peas, chicken, macaroni and cheese and roast
potatoes keep everyone coming to her house with Tupperware.
She bakes and decorates beautiful tiered fruitcakes for all the
family and church weddings and christenings and she can
make flowers out of icing sugar. Any time of day, Grandma
carries Extra Strong mints around. Sometimes she reads
romance novels. I know because I've seen them. She is always
on a healthy, healthy diet and eats tiny amounts of things out
of the smallest bowls, while everyone else is eating dinner.

Grandma shows me how to do a 'hospital corner' when
making the bed and I just can't get the hang of it. She gets
angry. Tells me I'm trying her patience. She says, 'Child, child.
Get it into your skull. Try not to be useless.'

Granddad is ever so particular. He is slim and sprightly, salt and pepper haired. Each time he learns a new word, he cross-references it in the *Oxford English Dictionary* and records it in his jotter, trying to use it in a sentence. He writes everything in capital lettering of equal size. He washes the dishes three times a day without fail, promptly after mealtimes. Every morning, he will have me quote English verses that he learned as a schoolboy in Jamaica.

'The heights by great men reached and kept,
Were not attained by sudden flight
But they, while their companions slept,
Were toiling upward in the night.'

'Don't lean on others! Be a man!
Stand on a footing of your own!
Be independent, if you can,
And cultivate a sound backbone.'

'Are these verses only for boys, Granddad?'
'No, child. It's just that man was made first.'
'Is that why you call me he sometimes?'
'Yes, child. Something we do from back home a' Jamaica. Man was made first, you see.'
'Does God think men are more important?'
'God doesn't think. God only knows.'
'So men are better than women?'
Granddad says he doesn't really want to put it like that, but woman was made from the rib of man,
     so,
   you know.

He takes to the bathroom, where he spends an hour deliberately washing his face and and trimming his beard each night after dinner. His copper shaving kit is gleaming, his routine precious. Cleanliness is next to godliness, says he. I want to be just like him. He has a place for everything and many wonderful, shiny cases . . . though not trinkets. Trinkets are terrible and decorative. Granddad's cases are definitely not decorative. They are definitely *only* containers.

Granddad has a few stock biblical answers for any question in the world
including

'There's a time and a place for everything under the sun.'

'Children obey your parents in the Lord.'

and

'Such is the way of this wicked world.'

I am not allowed to venture farther than the garden gate, unless to school or on church missions. Sleepovers are unnecessary and the cinema is terribly sinful.

'Halloween is nutt'n but Pagan Nonsense,' Granddad will spit, vexed to heaven. Then he will throw up his hands and say he doesn't know what this wicked world is coming to.

Other things that you definitely do not mention around him are:

— Prehistoric beasts or dinosaurs (which the Bible makes no mention of, and probably never existed)

— Anybody anywhere who ever says a swear word.

— Bacon.

— Films that are not about God.

Examples of those who are not God, Jesus or the Holy Spirit but are *Good* are:

1, Ellen G. White (who we have to learn about at church because she prophesied things about the end of the world and had spiritual visions)

2, The people in the Bible, mostly

3, Nelson Mandela

4, Dr Martin Luther King, Jr.

5, This man called Terry Waite (who was imprisoned as a hostage in Beirut for so long he forgot how to speak)

6, The pastor (and family)

We have many, many rules. Washing out the bath attentively and with intention,
   never forgetting to rinse. Wringing out the towels clockwise, anticlockwise, then clockwise again.
   Helping Grandma hand wash the clothes in the bath on a Sunday.
   Drinking bitters to purge the blood. Drinking bush tea to purge the blood. Drinking hot water to purge the blood. Attending prayer meetings to purge the soul.
   We sing lots of hymns with words like,
   'Wash me and I shall be whiter than snow.'

8.0

Gillibrand County Primary School was a sea of white, but for my black face. Despite that, I made friends. Mostly, if anyone tried to call me a name, at least two or three of them would rush to my defence. 'Don't be mean!' they'd shout. 'It's not her fault she's coloured! I'm telling on you.'

But at home, we were of the impression that the children at school were unruly and wild, and no example for good behaviour because they didn't respect anybody. And part of that,

it would be said,

is because white people put their babies on their fronts instead of their backs

(when everyone knows that a baby should be tied *behind* the mother so it can learn some respect).

According to Grandma, a lot of White People

Did not wash cups and plates properly (put them on the draining board full of soap suds)

Did not teach their children to clean the house. Let their children talk back at them.

Did not keep the Sabbath or care about God

Wore rips in their jeans and called it fashion

Couldn't cook too well, unless they were chefs

Went to pubs (terrible)

and ate food on tables with no tablecloths.

This of course did not apply to the white Jamaican couple at church, or the white couple from Scotland at church,
   or our nice next-door neighbour,
   or the doctor, or the insurance man.

One day, when Roo was visiting Grandma's for the summer holiday, there was a gentle knock at the door. Two earnest, wide-eyed Mormon boys had arrived, straining under their black suits in the sweltering July heat. One of them was blond and one mixed-race, and they spoke with American accents. They were both so pretty I was thinking they could have been on TV. I couldn't stop staring at them. We had to move all of our books out of the way so that we could set up a Bible study circle in the hallway. Grandma let us serve them fruit juice and ginger biscuits. Granddad was keen to discuss everything biblical. The blond one smiled gently at me and asked me about school. When I get a husband, I thought, I want him to look like either one of these two. I didn't mind which.

Things were going quite well, civil even, until there was a disagreement about the seventh day of the week, and the need to keep it holy.

Granddad was *livid*.

'The seventh day is the Sabbath of the Lord thy God! There it is! In black and white! Remember the seventh day to keep it holy! Six days shalt thou labour and do all thy work but the seventh day is the Sabbath of the Lord thy God!'

'Mr Daley, we . . .'

'Are you saying I don't know my Bible?'

'No, not at all, Mr Daley . . . I –'

'Dare you come into the house of a man of God and tell him that he doesn't know his Bible!'

'No, Mr Daley, that's not what we . . .'

Grandma was

almost nervous

'Daddy, calm down . . .'

'No, Mummy. These people are damn out of order.'

Little Roo and I looked at each other.

This was bad

really bad. (Both boys were flushed and uneasy.) Granddad was shouting at them as though they were

us.

'Let's just agree to disagree,' the brown one was saying, as they scrambled to their feet, in the direction of the front door. But there was no compromise to be met in a God-fearing house such as ours. They were thrown out

even before the biscuit crumbs settled on the carpet.

When Mum came home at the weekend to take Little
Roo, she sighed and said it might be better for him to change
nurseries. For him to stay a while at Grandma's,
  her being so busy with work
  and something called *stress*.

truth

Secret song for Linford James
aka *Dad*
by Little Roo and I.

'Dad is bad and we are mad
We are glad when Dad is sad
Dad is mad when we are glad
When we are sad, Dad is glad.'

Mum let us in on a new truth one evening. We were sitting in the back seat of her old white Sierra, waiting for the bingo hall to open so she could pick up her winnings. Once she had collected one hundred and fifty-seven pounds from the payouts desk and sat back behind the wheel, she sighed and lingered, one hand on the handbrake, the other running through her head of curls.

'You know Sonny?' she said, eyeing me in the mirror.

I nodded.

She tossed her head back towards Little Roo.

'That's his dad.'

Mum chewed and popped a stick of strawberry gum, staring into space. The car was filled with the smell of it.

A few years earlier, Sonny used to hang around our house from time to time, before disappearing into the ether. He was one of the DJs at the Caribbean Club, a gruff, stubbly 'uncle'. He spoke with a raspy voice and swore a lot. One night back then, when Mum was working a hospital night shift, he took me to work and left me to play on the dance floor.

'The baby is far too young to be in here,' a woman gasped. 'Have you no shame? That little girl ought to be in bed.'

'Fuck off,' said Sonny, who was standing by the DJ booth, drinking rum from the bottle. 'Find a man and mind your own damn business.'

Back in the car, Little Roo looked worried for a moment. 'I don't know Sonny.'

'No,' said Mum. 'Nobody does.'

My brother seemed happy with that. I went to say something, but Mum started up the car and asked me to please be quiet. She sang along to 'Mercy, Mercy Me' by Marvin Gaye. Couldn't carry a tune, though. Not for anything. We could barely hear ourselves think and by the time she had delivered us back to Grandma's, we'd forgotten all about Sonny.

That was, until the next time we saw Linford James – and told him the New Truth. We had run into him, quite by accident, one Saturday evening. We were playing on the kerb, waiting for Grandma to finish buying things at the store where they sold yam, plantain, green banana and hair relaxer. Grandma had to stock up after church on Saturdays in the next town, because you couldn't find black people's food or hair stuff where we lived. As we crossed over the road to the park, Linford was ambling up the street round the corner from our auntie's. He looked thinner than usual.

'Good evening,' we chorused, being well practised in politeness when it came to Big People.

'You two jus' bin a church?'

'Yep,' said Little Roo, sucking on a lollipop.

'Don't *yep* me, boy. How yuh like staying with Grandma, eh? You people is behaving yourself, now, isn't it?'

Little Roo fell silent for a moment and kicked up some dirt by the fence, pulling it into a mound of earth with the tip of his shoe.

'Stop doing that,' said Linford, 'those little shoes cost money, boy.'

'Yeah.'

'Yeaaa what? Don't get rude. Don't try my patience in this street today.'

My brother pulled his lollipop out of his mouth. The middle of his tongue was bright green.

'You're not my dad,' he said.

Linford's face made a hint of movement, a half-jerk.

'Who tell yuh dat?'

'Mummy,' said Little Roo. 'My real dad is Sonny. Sonny plays records at parties.'

'It's true,' I added. 'It's true. Mum said.'

Linford stared hard at us. He stood still for a while, working something out,
nodded
and told us both to take care. His voice was wet. We felt wrong, somehow.

We watched him float away and down the street, like dust.

This wouldn't do.

When we got home to Grandma's, I at once began to pen a letter to The Amazing Nigerian in pink, green and blue ink. I told him that we didn't know each other yet but according to Mum this was about to change. *According* was one of Granddad's favourite new words. I also used *apparently*, another new one.

I said that *apparently* I had brothers and a sister waiting for me with him in Africa and *apparently* one of them was the same age as me and that *according* to what I heard, Mum and I would take a trip in a few years, when it was *appropriate* (Mum's word) and we would meet everyone and we would all be together soon. I told him about my certificate for story reading and about the time I got called up in the school assembly and even the kids who didn't like brown people had to clap for me. I wanted to ask my father whether, all things considered, he might want to get back together with Mum and then I decided not to. I didn't want to get in trouble for being cheeky. My father would see me and know what to do. I had to have faith.

Little Roo supposed his real father, Sonny, to be some wild huntsman, from a different world. I made a note to share my father because Sonny never ever came to visit. Maybe Samson needed a father too.

Linford went away after the new truth, leaving his crinkled shirts hanging in one side of Mum's wardrobe and his tool box and shoes in the cupboard under the stairs. Mum wasn't the type to cry over things like this. Said she had a cold and that's why her eyes watered.

8.8

'Do you think,'
asks my brother,
hands on little hips,
'that Mum doesn't love us enough, and that's why we have
to live with Grandma and Granddad?'

We are going door to door collecting for World Wide
Advent Missions, selling images of thin, smiling African
children to the families in the neighbourhood. (My
grandparents and the church are behind this.) We are head to
toe in matching denim shirt and jeans sets.

I nod my head. 'I think she loves us a bit, but not as much as
other people's mums.'

'Is it because we're black? Granddad says that the world
hates black people.'

'No. Cos the people at church are brown and all of them are
with their mums. And Mum is brown too!'

'Granddad says we're black. Not brown.'

'Coal is black. Night and evil things are black. Brown
sounds nicer, Little Roo. Say brown.'

A teenager with deep-set eyes and a shaved head opens the
door and yells at whoever is in there that there are two Gollies
on the doorstep, before pounding up the stairs. The next thing
we know, the parents are staring down at us. In his sweet little
voice, my brother launches into a perfectly rehearsed,

'We're collecting for Adventist Trust. Would you like a
postcard or a fridge magnet?'

Their faces relax a little and they shake their heads no, but give us fifty pence each anyway. The lady is clutching a gold cross on a pendant around her stringy neck. They ask us if the children on the leaflets are people we know and we lie and say yes, they are all our cousins.

They ask us whereabouts in Africa we are from, but Little Roo doesn't know and I guess at *'Nigeria'* but I'm not sure if I said it right. We don't look like the children in the pictures, but the couple don't seem to notice.

The couple tell us our English is good and say they feel so very sorry for the Third World and all of its problems. 'It's because your leaders are corrupt,' the man says. 'They just won't govern themselves correctly. They want all the money and power for themselves and they don't give a toss about you people. Shame.'

We say thanks for the coins and when they shut the door, I'm feeling dark red things, and I don't know why.

I spin around to Little Roo and tell him that Mum is destined to go to hell,
straight to hell,
because she is a Jezebel who had children without being married and neither of us knows our fathers and that she's also a gambler because she goes to bingo and plays the National Lottery, which is a massive sin. I am angry with Mum a lot these days because we love her so much and we never see her. I am nearly halfway through the four years, but it has already been, like forever. On Sundays Little Roo and I stare out of the window, counting every white car that goes by, all the while hoping that she will come and pick us up and take us back home to stay.

This evening we make twelve pounds from the people in our area. The best day yet.

Even better . . . we get home and Mum is there!

There are tight knots in my tummy. There is wind in my body, whistling through the loops and twists. I can hear it. I want to seem mature and not too excited to see her standing here, but it is difficult. Difficult because she always feels like a dream.

I inhale. I blow out. I squeeze my buttocks together to stop the air escaping.

She looks

ah,

superstar brilliant. Her hair is shiny, past her shoulders

and she smells like strawberries. She has brought us a tub of Neapolitan ice cream to share. She spoons it out into two of the yellow bowls for us. Marcia's nails are shiny and red.

Grandma is hanging around with an odd expression on her face and says, 'Ice cream later. Marcia. Explain the ting to the child, nuh.'

Mum takes me upstairs to my room. Little Roo has to go and let Grandma bathe him, because it is almost dinnertime. 'What is a Golly?' he is asking her, as they disappear into the bathroom.

Mum says,

Get on the bed, sweetheart. She says she has something to tell me. *Something important.*

I am thinking,

I should never have thought or said those things about Mum.
We must be going back to live with her.
Maybe she loves us lots and lots and we just didn't know it.

My stomach is flipping out by now;
the wind in me is sighing and rumbling around my hip
area, wanting so much to escape. There are moths in my belly.
Pretty pink moths, darkening. When will she leave? Will it be
soon? I hope not. Marcia says I need to *listen carefully*
but I do not make it up onto my high bed before she lets it
drop.

'Your dad is dead,' she says.
'Not Linford. The real one.
Liver failure. Drank himself to death.'
She takes a spoonful of ice cream from my bowl.
'I so wanted him to meet his little girl. He would have loved
you.'

She bites at the scoop with her beautiful teeth.

All I can think is,
beauty makes everything bearable.

'You can't miss what you never had,'

says Granddad, over soup.

I put away the letter for Nigeria.

The Amazing Nigerian is dead. The Amazing Nigerian is

a total nightmare

Something strange is upon me. Everything is wrong. I wake up and the lightswitch won't work. Which is how I know Something Bad is Here. There is a frightening stillness in the black room. The curtains are a different colour. There is a red underlay to them and they are kind of glowing from outside. Which is how I know Something is Worse than Usual.

I look down at my small, tingling body. Everything feels wrong. Somehow I am already dressed for school and I might be late, because it is almost nine o'clock already. But it's dark outside, I think. My school uniform is as red, red as ever, melting, somehow seeping down on the floor beneath me and then we are standing in a graveyard. The teachers at school are there, crying, because Marcia was a good, good woman. She worked hard for you, they say. All those night shifts, they say, shaking their heads. She worked far too hard. And all you could do was be ungrateful. It is a grey, grey day. Mum is gone. Samson is holding my shoulders, telling me he must go back to the army.

From afar, Linford looks on.

We are standing at my mother's grave.

I wake up; heavy-lidded
Sore-throat-ed. My body hurts all over. Grandma takes my temperature,
gasps
and I get to miss school.

LITTLE ROO AND YRSA'S PLANS TO GET MUM TO TAKE US HOME ASAP — MEANING AS SOON AS POSSIBLE

1. Make everyone else poor like us. Turn the nightlights on at all of our friends' and cousins' houses so the electric bill is high and they'll be poor like us cos it's not fair that they have mums and we don't. 2. GET MONEY. Steal the glass Chandelier hanging in Auntie's hallway. Steal all of the crystals at the bottom first because they're tiny and Auntie won't notice and replace them with see-through plastic that you get on sweets. Sell the crystals at the market so Mum won't have to work nights. 3. Be ILL. So Mum will come with us to the doctor's.

8.9

Everyone is nervous and excited because Samson is home for a short while on army leave. I haven't seen my brother in ages and he's been fighting in Bosnia, Germany and Iraq. The last time I saw him was in the south of England when I was almost seven and we got there too late to see him awarded for his services to the Queen's Lancashire Regiment. All because Linford's pile-of-junk car broke down three times on the motorway. It was completely embarrassing.

I hide my teddy bears away in the cupboard and tidy my bedroom twice over, so that Samson will be impressed. Grandma says that because it's a Special Occasion, we can use the white lacy placemats instead of the plastic ones. I'm wearing my best cream satin skirt, which I usually save for church socials. I feel posh and grand. I could be a brown princess if I had nicer hair.

Samson arrives, grinning, with an open can of Coke for Roo and I to share. Samson is twenty-one now and when we go out to Chorley market, or shopping in the supermarket, girls whisper and giggle things about him. They say 'God he's gorgeous, he is' or 'what a fit black man' and I find it all so annoying. Ugh! He can do so much better than all of them! He loves pineapple, so Grandma puts pineapple pieces in with the jerk chicken and she makes homemade pineapple layered trifle.

I have written a poem at school for him

Before I start this poem
please may I introduce
my darling brother Samson
who loves pineapple juice

He joined the army five years ago
he's very big and strong
and if you think he's a coward
you're definitely wrong

I like him a lot
he's very kind and nice
he likes all kinds of food
especially rice

But as all poems do
this poem must now end
when I need him (all the time)
he's more than just a friend.

Samson reads the poem and bows his head for a second.
Then he sniffs and asks if he can keep it.
You're the brains of the family, you are, he says, folding up
the poem
 and placing it in his shirt pocket
 and I think I might diediedie from pride.

And you, kiddo, he says, turning to Roo. *You* are *pure talent*.

I want to be pure talent too.

I don't have poem brains or pure talent, says Samson. Just muscle and determination. And anger. And I can beat people up,

hahahahaha.

I know it's not true. Grandma keeps his old school exercise books and sometimes I read the stories he used to write about dragons, monsters and swashbuckling heroes.

But mostly, Samson is quiet. Mum keeps staring at him and beams at everything he says, but he doesn't look at her much. She is going crazy this week and is around a lot, hugging everyone. I love it, but Samson is not the hugging type, perhaps.

We all go to Mum's for the weekend and when Samson falls asleep, one long arm draped across me, I am so happy that I hardly dare breathe. I stare at his long eyelashes in the dark.

On Saturday afternoon, he brings this girl, Inessa, over to Mum's house. They are kissing for ages in Mum's car (Little Roo and I can't help but peep) and they sleep together in the bed in the next room and the bed makes noises through the wall and so do they. It gives me a funny feeling. I don't think I like her. Anyway, she doesn't talk much to us. I'm so happy when she leaves on Sunday morning and we get to have him all to ourselves again.

On Sunday evening, we are all sitting at the dinner table at Grandma's. We have just said grace and Samson's head shoots right up. He stares at our mother. Lays his clean knife and fork flat on the placemat in front of him.

Hey, Marcia. Do you remember throwing a chair at me when I was five? I wonder if you do, Marcia. I've never forgotten that.

There is a silence at the table and then, once everyone has eaten, Roo and I are told to find something to do upstairs. We can hear voices coming from below, but the only words that filter up are 'bad manners', 'army behaviour' and 'show some respect'. We strain to hear what Samson is saying, but we hear nothing.

When Samson leaves to go back to the army, everything is dead again. I don't speak to anyone for a week, not even at school

and I don't want to eat. I vomit into my cornflakes and my soup and three days later I have to go to the doctor's.

The doctor says I'm

distressed.

Grandma says

cut out the foolishness. Your brother will be back one day soon. It's nothing to make yourself sick over. Just focus on your schoolwork, you hear?

I don't know how to do that. Something burns my belly and will not shift.

9.1

Two new boys arrive at our school. Arthendu and Sajib from Bangladesh!

They are cousins and their skin is almost the same colour as mine. It's completely wonderful. Friends, maybe?

But they're quiet and don't make friends with anyone else because they're still learning about England. The teachers say we need to give them space to get *comfortable*. Their mothers sometimes come to school with them and help with the school dinners and in art class.

Sajib and Yrsa should get married, sing my friends.

Sajib and Yrsa should get married.

Dear Sajib,

Did you have a girlfriend back
home? I think that you are beautiful
and we can be brown things together.
My friends say I should like you. And I do.
Lots of like!
Let's see where this goes!

It was the worst thing in the world. These people had me
cornered.
On the dining-room table, my grandparents slammed down
the screwed-up letter that I lost the nerve to send
and tried to throw away.
'You love that boy, do you? Do you?' Granddad was
shouting.
'Hear me, and hear me well. Don't you ever. In this life.
Push yourself up on a boy.
Don't you ever write a note like that again . . . to anyone!
You hear me?'
Grandma was softer, but only a little.
'If a boy sees you and likes you, he will tell you. Don't you
ever. In this life. Approach men.
It is not nice, it is not good,
and they will not thank you for it.
A man gets to see what he likes and asks for it. That's the way
it goes.'

The following week, my P.E. teacher was joking with me
when Granddad came
to collect me.
'It's a leap year this year!' he said with a broad teacher smile.
'That's when the girls ask the boys out, eh?'
Mr Tyrell was a jolly English man
and could not know that this was terrible timing
after the blizzard in our living room one week prior.
I said nothing. Granddad said less.

9.5

It wasn't fair. Mum always said we couldn't afford anything. Unless it was a book. Or something to do with school or education. Mum always said, 'I'm doing everything on my own. Have some understanding. I have to give money to Grandma to pay for things, so SHOW SOME RESPECT.'

Marcia was stressed too about all the times we were spending at the hospital these days. The X-ray showed my bones were growing too fast for my muscles, and I had to wear ugly knee supports. My knees and shins ached after I walked up the hill to school and back home. Even with knees that hurt, I had been excited about Junior School Sports Day for weeks. But on the day itself it rained, which meant it had to be postponed. Nobody told the parents though. At one o'clock a small number of parents was gathering in the rain and I could see my mum, alone, towards the back. From the classroom, I watched our head teacher run out with his umbrella to tell them all that it was not going to happen because of the weather. What an awful waste of time.

Mum looked so tired. She was in the middle of a solid two and a half weeks of night shifts at Chorley hospital during the weekdays and Manchester hospital at the weekends. She didn't see me watch her walking slowly back to the car on the grass. Her pink shell suit was inside out. I was praying to God that no one noticed. She passed by my class window but I didn't wave. I felt a flurry of pity and sadness. She'd dragged herself all that way to school for nothing.

My best friends were Ellen and Annika, two sisters a year apart from each other. Every so often, Grandma would allow me to go to their house for tea now that I was almost ten. Their house was sunny and large and they had a Packard Bell computer in their home office and pink wallpaper in the twin bedroom they shared with matching princess nets over the bed.

At dinner time we had alphabet spaghetti and cheese on toast instead of awful things – like yam and rice and beef – that I had to eat at home.

One night, over dinner, Ellen and Annika's mum placed a bejewelled hand on mine, right there at the table and leaned towards me, her brow furrowed.

Perhaps, when you change, lovie, you'd like to get dressed for P. E. in the girls' bathroom, or perhaps you'd like to leave your vest on, she said in a low, conspiratorial whisper.

You are a little more developed than the others she said.

with an odd smile. Would you like me to speak with your teacher?

It was so annoying. I wanted to die, right there at the table Adults everywhere were always saying horrible things with smiles. I longed for smallness; to be petite. To have small hands and feet and no growing pains; no angry lion dreams and definitely no boobs. On my eighth birthday I had wished hard to look like everyone else and I was already nine and could not see it happening yet. I felt my eyes begin to fill and held the tears back. I looked across at Ellen and Annika, who hadn't heard a thing, and were busy playing with each other's hair. Right at the dinner table.

Grandma and Granddad would not have stood for that for a minute. This evening, the sun hit their blonde ponytails and they each looked exactly like spun gold.

That night I dreamed I had a large sun-filled house with a computer and pink walls.

Mum was still my mum, of course, but my dad was a white man and called me the most beautiful girl in the world.

9.6

Our family doctor is peering at me.

'I don't really know what she's talking about, Doctor,' says
Grandma,

'But every so often the child comes out with the same thing,
over and over again. It's causing me worry.'

Dr Melling has the softest, whitest hands you have ever
seen, and his office is chock-full of toys. A yellow teapot filled
with miniature people, a Rubik's Cube, jigsaws. He must be a
wonderful dad, I think. I feel my stomach get all funny.

'What do you mean, you *don't feel real*? Try and put it a
different way for me,'
he says with a kind chuckle.

But there is no word to describe the feeling of disappearing
and being there at the same time.

I want him to place his hands on my head again, as though
I'm his girl or something, and I don't know why. Must
concentrate. Grandma is frowning at me.

'Is it true that you're seeing patterns?'
he says. 'Cartoons? Flickering lights too, you say, like snow?'
'Only at night,' I say,
'only at night.'

'And your knees are still hurting you once you've walked
home from school?'

'Yes, quite a lot.'

Dr Melling prescribes some painkillers.

'And you're still getting a sick stomach each Saturday before
church?'

'Talk up, child,' says Grandma, suddenly irritated.

'Yes, stomach ache.'

Dr Melling prescribes a laxative.

It doesn't really work; any of it. My heart is in my teeth when we pull up each Saturday outside the church building to go into Sabbath School. The girls my age laugh at my clothes and ask me why my hair is so bad. They tell me my shoes look old and the hair tie is babyish. They ask me if the damp smell in the room is me. It could be.

Their ringleader, 'Alyssa' makes me dread Saturdays. It is easily the longest day of the week. When I walk into a room they stop talking and stare. I am surprised, because I look just like these girls, so why am I lonelier here than at school? Also, it is not Christian to be mean to someone and make them feel bad. Some weeks they sit a row behind me, talk, laugh, point. 'We don't like you,' they say. 'Your clothes are so sad and you look as though you were just dragged through a bush. Your hair needs straightening or extensions or something.'

'Don't you have an iron between you?'

'Why do you live with your grandparents? Don't you have a mum and dad?'

'Does your grandma make your clothes? It looks like it.'

'Why do you and your brother walk funny?'

I sit by myself and pretend not to hear and talk to the elders who are always telling me to smile.

The weeks go by though, as weeks do. You can always rely on time.

Also, I learn what not to feel.

a weekend at Mum's

We get to miss church on Mum's birthday because she says
we need to spend more time together!

Mum, Little Roo and I are so happy to be together we lay
down watching Disney films, and looking at each other and
touching each other's hands, noses and eyelashes. Mum combs
out my hair and oils my scalp with the green Dax Wax. It
hurts but you grit your teeth. You think of something else. Or
you swallow a painkiller and take another for Good Measure.
That's what I do for the knee pain. I love my knee tablets.
They're tiny and sweet, like mints, and kind of fizz on your
tongue. Mum tells us how much she loves having us home.
Her eyes are shining. I hug Little Roo in front of me. I can get
my arms all the way round him. We drink cream soda (YES!!)
and eat sausage and chips at lunchtime,

even though sausage is bad

(because, in the Bible, one day all the pigs got possessed by
demons and drowned themselves). If you are a God-fearing
Christian you can definitely not eat disgusting swine

but the sausage tastes amazing, sweet and juicy. I swallow
them quickly and promise God I'll never sin again. We want to
stay here forever. Mum even lets us have sweets before dinner

but

there is red on the landscape.
Linford comes to visit.

I am swallowing some hot tea and Linford walks into the house, just like that. We haven't seen him since we told him what we knew. Mum regards us nervously.

'Linford misses you,' she says. 'Come, we're going out for Chinese.'

I go hot

and the wrong kind of tingly.

Linford nods in our direction but does not smile.

'Get your coats on, kids,' he growls.

our day out

mum has won at bingo cos she's back with maccy d's
she smells a bit of smoke
but no one really minds
it feels just like a holiday
the very best kind
she lets us stay up late. She got two nights off work.
She smiles at Linford /Halfling Dad
she smiles at me
our halfdad smiles back and we look like a family
mum is feeling good and we do too.
She asks us where we want to go the very next day
and we choose Blackpool Theme Park the world's best place
for pink and blue candyfloss and popcorn that's gone soft.
Our halfdad's in a mood again but mum says just ignore him
run along enjoy yourselves but don't get lost
and do not speak to strangers
unless they look like us
haha
she laughs to herself, she's tired but amused
she carries all the bags, she needs new shoes
she smiles at our halfdad
and Linford looks away
and I just really hope that she's having a nice day.

10.0

Since Linford appeared at the window on the ladder,
since the night our unicorn came and left,
something is happening with my brother and windows at
night. He no longer reads stars,
not at all,
and has lost all interest in the moon and its cycles. He will
not even approach a window, let alone peer out of one. Neither
Grandma nor Granddad have noticed, but I see something
come over Little Roo at a certain time around sunset,
some inward tremble, when his face appears to shrink
against the softening light.

Something is also happening concerning how I feel about
mirrors, at precisely the same time. I know what I look like,
secondhand. Adults say *pretty*. I cannot fathom this. My
reflection looks to me like lines and circles that I can't work
out. Large eyes and too much limb and thickness and black
black skin and there are several contradictions in the dark. I do
not look in the mirror for fear of several things. I sleep in the
large back room with the lumpy paper and woodchip ceiling.
I am old, I know, too old to be afraid of mirrors at night, but
mirror land is unpredictable at the best of times. Perhaps the
daytime reflection may be late travelling back and I might
catch a glimpse of the thing in its place, staring back at me.

Yes, mirror land is unreliable. All that separates the two worlds is a thin pane of glass, and that's no comfort. Who knows where one ends and one begins? Glass won't keep the dark out. Ask Little Roo.

Worse— Maybe I'm the danger. Perhaps the black shape in the dark is me.

Evidence 1

(the looking glass)

The girl is perhaps too young for this. She stands, tall for her age, in the large window in the room with the woodchip and lumpy wallpaper.

It overlooks her grandparents' garden with the cabbage patch and the turnips
and Granddad's shed
and the next-door neighbour's garden and greenhouse.

The neighbours are standing in the garden, drinking cups of black coffee.

She angles her naked body so they would be able to see . . .
if they stopped talking and
looked up right now
if one of them just flicked up their eyes
if . . .

her breathing is changing
she feels it warm, rumbling
building, below the belly
down through to her toes
her legs start to tremble
and

there it goes

she shudders
rests two hands on the cool glass. Her toes cling to the
carpet.
The mirror sees all, misses nothing.

Evidence 2

(the window)

A boy is sitting on the floor,
  playing with his toy cars
when he feels his throat close up. He realizes that the room
is growing dim. His chest is thick, anxious. The Night, he
understands, is a wild, wild time. He knows that as a boy, he
must be tough. Granddad would kill him if he knew he was
scared . . . of a window? How very silly.
  Come on. Got to be tough.
  They have this song at church about Daniel in the Bible, and
how brave he was. How he stood in the lion's den and nothing
happened to him, because of COURAGE and PURPOSE
  Dare to be a Daniel, says the song
  Dare to be a Daniel.
And all the men stand up, singing, thumping the little boys
enthusiastically on the backs as they do. But Daniel was living
in old times, before there were gunmen and tanks and serial
killers on the ITV news. Plus
  there is the thing his sister told him once,
  this thing she said could
  would
  might happen
  if/when he was naughty. This thought that he can't ever seem
to shake.
  'If you are bad . . .
  only IF you are bad,

the back wall behind your headboard opens up as you sleep
and you sink back into the wall on a conveyor-belt thing
(your bed and all)
to the underworld
to hell, where there is the devil himself and imps, goblins
and wailing things, too horrible to imagine.
You will be cremated alive
while the goblins laugh and play in the distance.' If all this is
true, he thinks,
and it must be
because his big sister told him and his big sister would never
lie
so
if the Bible and these horrible tales are true . . . you can't take
chances with windows. Who knows what you might find
scaling the brickwork
to find you cowering, smaller than ever? Whether you are in
a high-rise block or a basement flat, you'd be a fool to look
out. Who knows what could be waiting? Snakes on the ground
or the devil on a ladder.

pink / yellow

At first, it looked like a dream.
Little Roo and I were standing in Grandma's pink pink
bathroom.
It was a Friday night/Saturday morning
a holy day. The Sabbath.
He was clutching at his bedsheet in horror. He'd had
another accident.
It was happening every night, without fail. 'I don't want to
get beaten,' he said, crying.
Grandma and Granddad were mad as anything about it
and said they would knock him into next week each time it
happened
but he couldn't stop.
It was early in the morning and they were still asleep.
We were fear-filled, and rightly so.
We got the salt water and the Disinfectant
and we sponged all of the piss from the plastic sheets.
But Grandma woke
Grandma got up
Grandma walked across the hallway
and said, 'Stop locking this door, you hear? What are you
people doing?'
'Nothing', we said, pushing the plastic sheeting in the wash
basket.

'Nothing', we said, bunching the bedsheet under the rug, in panic. Roo's little hands were sweating.

I opened the door. By then, the plastic sheeting was hidden, out of sight;

the wet bedsheet was forced into the Fourth Dimension. The bathroom, still very very pink.

Were we dreaming? No.

'Better be nothing,' said Grandma's figure in the doorway.

10.1

Beauty makes people stay, I thought. Beauty makes people listen to you. Beauty makes people fall in love with you and not know what to do with themselves. It was in all the songs and it was in the Disney films. It was even in the Bible. Song of Solomon, my favourite book of the Bible so far, was all about beauty and lovers and love. I couldn't wait till my life changed and I looked more like a thing that people liked. The boys at school made a list of the most beautiful girls in the class from 1 to 15. I did not make the list but that's because they all agreed that I didn't need to

because I was more of A Cool Black Friend,

not a girlfriend, you understand

but a Cool Black Girl Friend

with spongy hair that was dead cool.

I had been praying for beauty for two years straight, with no real success, no concrete results. No one could see it unless they were adults, so I made plans. After all, there was lots I could do to facilitate this.

Plan one. Ask Grandma about hair relaxer. Or a perm. The white girls used Pantene Pro-V in their hair. I needed to get hold of that and mix it with our horrible shampoo to make my hair come out straighter, shinier, LONGER.

Plan two. Do exercises every day from Grandma's yoga book and DO NOT EAT TOO MUCH.

That meant NO CRISPS, DESSERTS,

only GRANDDAD'S DIABETIC BISCUITS when he shares them.

Buy *Sugar* and *Bliss* magazines to learn tips on how to attract boys.

Use Mum's hair gel for shine. Dream/idol look:

Kelly Kapowski from *Saved by the Bell*
or
Pamela Anderson
or one of the Sweet Valley High twins.

Only a tiny amount of people will enter the kingdom
of God, says the Bible. Only a small section will be saved
from the fires of damnation; that is to say, those who take
the narrow road and work hard and worship God and are
hard-working and modest. Children of the Lord who do
everything right. Each time we got on our knees to pray in
church I began to cry, because I wasn't sure that I would ever
make it to heaven. The Bible said we come into the world as
sinners. Perhaps I just wasn't a good enough person to turn
it all around. I wanted to have long shiny hair and read
magazines for girls and wear pink lipgloss and short skirts and
be completely adored and wanted and loved;
I was sure of the heaven in that.

wildlife

I am moving around, slowly, with intent,
underneath my Very Best Friend. We are 'practising for
boys', you see. An important and necessary task. We call this
sex thing 'snakes and elephants',
so no one finds us out when we refer to it at school. Code
words are everything.
This friend is mean to me sometimes, at school. But never
when we're in bed. Never ever in bed.
After it's finished,
after we have acted just like wildflowers
daisy headed,
after we have rubbed together in the wind, somewhat
been as dandelion clocks, drifting
summer tuliped
buttercupped
come away; once our inner petals are softened
we go downstairs. I reek of her. She is a petite girl and my
T-shirt totally drowns her. My insides still ache with longing.
She is on my skin. I want more
so much more,
but it's dinner time
i.e. we have been summoned.

We sit down to rice and chicken
and I really really think I could be in love
i.e. not 'practising for boys',
not really, not ever.
Grandma and Granddad know nothing, of course. They are
talking over our heads about how someone's eighteen-year-old
daughter at church is pregnant and not even married!
This thing we've been doing, my Very Best Friend and I,
this feels right; feels free. Like life could be completely new.
I feel like myself, stronger. Like the warrior me. As though I
could take on an army. Strong like Samson.
Dashing like Samson. I wish I was Samson. No boobs, just
strong and kinglike and black.
Some distant soldier. A wonderful mirage. A thing that all
the girls love.

The news hit us. Linford was living with Auntie Lizette. Mum's best friend.

Linford went and moved in with Auntie Lizette. Mum's best friend.

Linford and Auntie Lizette AKA the Best Friend of Mum. Auntie Lizette? Linford? Our jaws dropped.

Auntie Lizette was brown and plump with a silky curly perm, and plum frosted lips.

Auntie Lizette and Mum stopped speaking, unless they saw each other in the street or at Carnival or something. Then they would nod hello to each other, keeping it moving. We were warned to be polite if we ran into her though, because children were to be respectful at all times, with no exception.

'Leave them to it,' Mum said, tossing her head, drinking her brandy tea.

'I would never have expected it, but leave them to it.

And be wary of friends, yeah? They are the ones who will kill you, in the end.'

everything else

Wishes do come true after all. I was eleven when Little Roo
and I were able to live with Mum again. She had moved into
the area and lived a fifteen-minute walk away from Grandma's,
opposite the cemetery and right next door to my high school.
Being back with Mum was such a relief. We could exhale. So
we did.

Mum had a microwave and cable TV, chocolate in the
cupboard, Bakewell tarts, ready-made apple pies and a plastic
electric kettle with no whistle
(we were tired, by then, of the whistling). Everything was
plastic and modern and we could warm up our delicious ready-
meals in minutes. Pictures of Jesus did not adorn the walls
and there were no cabinets filled with china, although she did
leave the wrapping on the chairs, like all the other Jamaicans
we knew. She was still working night shifts at Manchester
hospital and would return home at eight the next morning,
exhausted. In the daytimes, Mum would try to catch up on her
growing deficit of sleep while we were at school. We would see
her around six to seven p.m. as she prepared for the night shift
again. She did her best.

Mum didn't like to throw things away reader's digest books
stethoscopes sellotape old high school jotters stained pieces of paper
monopoly pieces and the fake money photographs pens that didn't write the
bingo card perfume bottles old plant food tomato sauce sachets mustard
in case someone needed it kfc after dinner wipes old credit cards keys to
boxes long forgotten tea stained cloth the sewing kit plasters and bandages
from 1984 old surgical gloves pills we didn't know the name of painkillers
antiinflammatories antihistamines vitamin capsules cod liver oil rust filled
biscuit tins plastic money boxes stress balls shells from Blackpool beach
nuts bolts and screws recipes scrawled on old magazine covers letters from
Jamaica postage stamps photos of Samson and we could not keep our
house well. Everything was in disarray. Cobwebs grew in the
corners of the ceilings and there was grime on our skirting
boards and door handles. Grassy weeds sprung up from the
gaps in the windowsills. Mould grew in cups and mildew on
old clothes on the floor. The garden was a junkyard.

We ate store-bought ready meals in boxes, rice and chicken
and party food, unless Grandma sent fish and chicken,
macaroni and cheese or rice and peas in Tupperware boxes.

We were not inclined to cleaning, even after all of the
meticulous attention to detail we had been taught. Especially
after that. At Grandma's, wiping our faces in the hand towel
would earn us a slap. At Mum's, Little Roo and I could do
what we wanted. So we did.

Grandma and Granddad despaired over the state of the
place,

but it was out of their hands.

At night I was entrusted to put Little Roo to bed at seven forty-five and retire myself at a time I deemed reasonable. It took a while to settle into this new lifestyle of freedom. Apart from medical journals, her cabinets were full of Mills & Boon romance novels and sex booklets.

Great Sex,

Sexpectations (a tale of lusty romance)

and an illustrated *Kama Sutra*. My favourite picture was entitled 'The Only Way for Women to be Together'. I dog-eared the page and tucked it behind my pillow every night.

Roo would read anything he could find, too. He would pore through the medical journals like a little professor and he learned to pick up most church songs by ear. He could mimic all the cartoon character voices and strained his eyes by sitting too close to the TV until he had to wear glasses. We memorized the words to everything we watched and read and made brightly coloured picture books out of scrap paper, felt tips and Samson's old comics from the eighties. We had a radio show that we would record on my cassette recorder and we made plans to get famous and live in a house with all the computer games, sweets and books we could dream of.

physics and magic

Every night around ten pm they play reruns of this old, old show from back in the day called *Quantum Leap*. In the show, Scott Bakula aka Dr Sam Beckett travels through space and time in just a matter of seconds. Mum has a book of magic in her front room, sandwiched between the Bible and the non-illustrated *Kama Sutra*. A powder blue hardback book from the *School Of Divine Power* about 'jumping timelines', documenting various scientists who say that you can jump into whatever reality you can conceive with positive activations.

Just think, says the book, these are all your lives, happening right next to each other, and you get to choose your frequency.

Meaning dimensions are very very real.

Meaning Roo and I did see a unicorn last year.

Meaning we were absolutely Not dreaming.

So beauty is coming. Money is coming. Fathers are coming. The book says that time is an illusion, a bendable concept. Unreal. So maybe as you are reading this I am already twenty nine or fifty or something, or two and still reading on the worktop with Mummy. I am also very unmistakably here and you are so unmistakably there – only we aren't. We are anywhere we want to be

and if that beautiful actor Scott Bakula can travel through time, collapsing the old timelines in seconds, I bet we could even travel diagonally. I can see my father, or something like that, and stop him from going back to Nigeria (although I wouldn't want my brothers and sister to be without him).

Maybe he could travel backwards and forwards in time and they won't notice him gone!

Mum says I might be mixing concepts and not to think about this so much and also not to mix the actor Scott Bakula with his character Sam but she is always tired and not a good person to discuss this with. *Quantum Leap* is the best thing on television, in my opinion. Scott aka Sam travels through space and time because he accidentally stepped into some time vortex or cupboard or something when it wasn't ready. I feel for him. As soon as he gets comfortable he gets blasted to another set of bad circumstances in a different space and time and he has to rely on his friend Al to guide him through the dodgy situation in order to stop the bad thing in history from happening,

which makes me so, so happy before I go to bed. I have moved through several timelines already, I think. Time is an illusion, say the scientists. It is molecular, it is bendable or liquid, it is soldered metal;
or it is droplets of memory. I imagine it looks like mercury, silver and illusive.

The powder blue book is amazing. I love magic science. The book takes a dim view on the West and its trapping, limiting concept of time. Burn all the clocks. I am free. My friends can come to call for me at night and there is no more church on Saturdays and Linford has gone on his merry way. My Very Best Friend is a droplet of chemical memory as well. Our timeline has totally collapsed. She is trying to spread rumours about me all the way over at another school, miles away, calling me a lesbian. I don't care. If Scott Bakula A K A Sam can jump from the future to a nightclub in the sixties to being sheriff of a small town in the forties to teaching Michael Jackson the moonwalk, I can deal with a mean deadweight disappearing from my life. There are always new people to touch and be touched by. I have just started high school for God's sake, where the real stuff is about to begin, and I am too excited at this moment in time to be missing my Very Best Friend or anyone else. It's just as Mum says. Be wary of friends. Anyway, I have more important things to be concentrating on, like Growing Up. High school will be everything. I am porous I am bold. I am a space-time travelling expert.

I am close to twelve, you know (in theory;
in your Western linear time concept at least)
and this is how it goes.

TWO

12.0

This is how it goes.
You start having sad days. Get to know what 'going under' is.
Going under is when everything
feels pitch grey. You crave something
but you don't know what. The boys at high school are juvenile,
small and rude. The girls at school flirt with the boys at school.

Samson gets married. The whole family travels down South
to the wedding on a Friday. He is marrying a pretty girl
from near London. She has lots of tattoos and is lovely and
everything
but you can't stop crying at the wedding. It feels so much like
the end of things.

'You are erratic' says your mum, often.
'What's wrong with you? What are these black moods?'

You feel your body temperature sinking
feel tired all the time
sweat too much
stop washing. You read *Joy of Sex*
the man looks like
Christ but you ignore Jesus these days
you want love these days
you imagine what sex must be like

and know you must find out.
So you can't leave the earth just yet.

13.0

One day
two builders whistle at you in the street.
Oi, sexy!
Ello, gorgeous!
It's a feeling you
haven't had before
something prickly and bright.
Power. Fear.

13.2

feel fat
feel fat
stop washing
feel

Little Roo says,
'I don't think you're fat.'
You sigh and hate yourself
in the mirror.

13.9

or
how it begins

Your friend's dad likes
to joke about the length of your legs
asks why you're not a supermodel yet.
Tells you he's sure you'll go far if you try.
You like the look in his eyes when
he says it.

14.0

Your friend's dad is looking at you
Your friend's dad likes you. Your friend's dad says
Look . . . I can't have you walking home at this hour. Put your
bike in the back of my car and I'll
take you. There is musk in his voice. Just like that, something
shifts
and you know something
and he knows something
but nobody knows for sure. You have something to trade
and you're not sorry. Smile back at your friend's dad in the
rear view mirror
hold his gaze, daunting as that might be. Let him drive you
home (again)
and let him say (again) that you've got legs that go on forever
notice – it takes him twenty minutes to drive you home

when you live ten minutes up the street
feel good about that.
Know that he wants to be around you.
Play into the powerfear. Pretend you dropped your purse
and stretch out on the back seat like a cat
smile at his confusion in the dark
then say 'thank you' and bolt quickly
soon as he pulls up to your front door, before he
has time to do or to think a thing. Before he has an *issue*. Feel
funny when you get in the house. And relieved. The wrong
kind of tingling.
Make an excuse the next time he wants to drive you home.
With a pert black body
and a wet, wet mouth
maybe
anyone's dad can be yours. You're the danger.

14.2

Meet Terence
Mum's boyfriend
who cheats on her but is otherwise fine
good to talk to. A laugh, sometimes, if he's in a good mood.
Little Roo does an excellent impression of Terence. Puffs out
his chest and puts on a deep voice. Terence is always slicking
his curls with wet-look gel and playing with his moustache.
Twirling it around like a classic villain. Little Roo could be an
actor if he wanted. The master of impersonation. Cheeks out
like Terence, walks with his belly sticking out.
Terence has Nike trainers
says he'll pick you up a pair
Terence likes R & B. You get into R & B

feel like a girl from the video
realize you
could
look like a girl from the video
Get long hair, soft long waist-length
braids that make you look
like something lovely.
Little Roo says you look like a princess.
Thank him on the way out. You don't have time to stay in and
watch TV shows with him anymore. There are things to do
and people to see. Go to the off licence, brazen as anything, to
buy booze for your friends and anyone else who asks.
Always get served; anyone would swear you're at least twenty.
Huddle up with the gang on park benches in the bitter
northern winter
drinking cider, talking shit, sharing cigarettes. There is a blond
boy who curses and spits a lot
and never looks at you. You're scared if you catch his eye.
Disappointed when you don't.
One night he places a head on your lap, drunk.
'You're alright, you know, kind of pretty.
I don't mind Coloureds; it's the pakis I hate.'

14.3

Pose naked for a strange man in the next town
who says he can shoot portfolios. He tells you
you could be the next Naomi. Alec. Any
one of them other black *lasses*.
He says you'll do well because your nose is 'nice and slim'.

read your mum's diary that she does not keep private.
She records days that she has sex with smiley faces.
Plus, there are the days underlined in red
see . . . *Jan 20th*
Found Terence in bed with his white woman
see . . . *Feb 11th*
New glasses for the kids.
see . . . *Feb 26th*
Gynaecologist

meet David, mum's new boyfriend
who steals money from her
and asks you if you've done it with a boy yet.
Hear David having sex with her
feel weird.

Find the problem page
in *Sugar* magazine
I hear my parents having sex!
Paper-clip it to a letter for your mother and leave it in her
handbag.
notice the louder noises subside for a while, but then she
forgets. It starts up again and you feel sick
but *interested*
but sick
. . . hate David!
hear her tell her friend Madge
David is no good in bed. Feel a little better.

feel no blood inside of you
find concentrating hard
cry in frustration in Maths
read ahead in English
drift, mostly
hold the gaze of male teachers for too long
feel them react
feel the powerfear
pluck your eyebrows into questions
and
roll your skirt up at the waist

Meet Devonte outside the Red Lion pub.
He's a black man with a black name in this white town. You
exhale. What a find! Someone to match you. Devonte is
beautiful, with large dark eyes.
It's weird, he says. You're the same age as my sister
but she's just a kid.
Give him your number. Invite him into your room
two days later
in the day, when your mum is sleeping
let him on top of you,
nearly inside
and when asked if you've ever done this
before
feel very shy about the fact that you haven't, so
lie. Which is a mistake.

When it's over and you're downstairs
feel awful; sore/awful
on fire; rude fire

and wonder how anybody ever enjoys that
ever.
Pretend not to notice him stealing four CDs on the way out.
They belong to David anyway
who is

awful
it hurts
it hurts to sit.
you smell
different. There's a weird scent
about you
some male odour. The man left his smell behind
all over you. You ache.
You lie in bed a lot.
Roo comes to sit with you sometimes. Sits at the end of the bed
reading his comic and swinging his legs. Wants to be a
Superhero these days.
Always there just to be there. He puts a hand on your forehead
'Are you sick?' he whispers,
concern behind his little red-framed glasses.
'I think so. Yes,'
you say
and turn to the wall.

Go under
feel cold all the time
feel you don't see the point of life.
One night
Mum walks in when you're in the bath.
'Stand up now,' says she. 'Look in the mirror

and look hard.
You want to die? Are you crazy?
You're the most beautiful thing I made.'

Go under. Far under.
notice more odd things about David
e.g.
mood swings
(some days he really hates you)
e.g.
an obsession with young black female singers
e.g.
an
obsession with cookies
cakes
and other sweet things
e.g.
when he finds out you like strawberry milk bottle sweets
he buys you a carrier bag full of them.
Too many to eat. Like two hundred
e.g.
tells you and your mum how pretty you both are
how he's a lucky man
What happened to that Devonte?
he mocks,
Devonte seemed nice.

You
sneak out at the weekend.
Down beers in bars. Talk to men who tell you they're
married, but it's not fun anymore

it's all going to shit, they say.
She doesn't understand me, they say.
I only stay because of the kids,
or
It's just something about you, they say.
Let them feel you up a little
at last orders and again on the way home through the park. Let
them stick their tongues in your mouth
it's a little bit awful (especially if they're old)
but not the worst. The Worst is doing nothing. Letting life sink
in.
Take a job washing dishes in some Italian restaurant
the men:
Santino, waiter
Mario, owner
Marco, chef
Marco says
Listen,
I want to go out with you.
What do you think, says Mario
About coming out with me?,
I want you to teach me English, says Santino
Play into the powerfear
consider all of them,
even though Mario is old and pot-bellied
and Marco's wife hired you
You're going to the park to teach a grown man English?
says David.
There's a name we used to have for girls like you.
Prick tease.
David smirks. His teeth are terrible.

the girl and the cleaner of glass

Although this is all her body,
all five foot nine and three quarters of it,
the girl doesn't recognize it as such. As anything other than
(1) *a Hot-thing* (2) *a weapon of delicious and complete
destruction* (3) *an almost-power*. The usual window cleaner is
away on holiday. The new man is chirpy, with an accent from
down South. Kind of draws out the vowels. Sounds different,
like someone from the telly.

He has just finished all the windows and he asks if there's
anyone else home
and for some reason the girl says,
'Just me, shall I pay you?'
even though it's not strictly true – her mum is crashed out
upstairs, knackered from the night shift and the day shift and
the night shift and David is at the video game store and could
walk through the door any minute. Little Roo is in the living
room, glued to the Cartoon Network. None of that matters. She
twists two of her braids between her long fingers.

'I like your hair,' says the window cleaner, on cue. 'Really
pretty.'
'And so,' he says, 'is the rest of you.'
She's teasing, to begin with. Sits on the kitchen table
swinging her long, long legs. It's supposed to be a game, a trick
to help her catch her reflection.

He waltzes over. Like a cowboy in a Western. There is power
and there is fear and they are staring right at each other.

He is bright-eyed and adept and surprisingly prepared and
even though they're in the kitchen

and there is no introduction to what is about to happen
he gets it out right there and then
and slides on a yellow condom. Yellow, she thinks. Ha,
Yellow, she thinks
My favourite colour as a kid
Yellow, she thinks
Shit, I used to be a kid.
Yellow;
am I still

a . . .

and all this is a little unexpected but she's a grown-up
girl, whatever. At this point, she thinks, it's weird not to. It
happens; perhaps it hurts,
but anyway. It doesn't take long.
It happens on the kitchen table, which is odd. What a
woman, he says, indulgently, shaking his head as he leaves.

She thought she saw herself watching from outside,
in the awful garden.

I'm sure I'll make it into his dreams, she thinks, and takes two showers.

16.0

It is summer.

She is walking in the woods round the back of the school with
Dylan.
They sit on a bench in the clearing. Dylan is from the estate
round the back and is hazel-eyed and almost red-haired but
not quite. They start kissing, because it has been on the cards
for, like, ever. She opens up his fly because it's what you do.
Kiss it, he says, so she does. Over and over again
until he finishes. He tells her thank you.
She feels power and sex, like she knows what she is made for.
At home, David has made bland awful pasta. With green
awful pesto.
At home, David asks her where she went.
She says
'school'
and he glares and says,
'Really. School.
Really.'
'Leave it alone, David. For once,'
snaps Mum, exhausted,
leaving for work.

let's do something together

David has a friend, Peter,
a filmmaker who works in a video store. Peter is witty and greying,
large stomached, green-eyed. Sees David for the idiot he is.
Apparently David hangs around the store all day and all the men make fun of him behind his back.
Apparently David brags about his stepdaughter who can sing better than most of them on TV and is bound to be famous.
Peter comes over to see David and Mum one night.
They all sit in the living room
laughing loudly
eating Pringles, drinking white wine and watching DVDs.
Peter says he can make you a demo CD for all the record companies.
You go to the studio.
You sing for Peter. Toni Braxton and Whitney Houston and Des'ree
with karaoke backing music.
'I really like your voice,' Peter says, 'And I think that I could get you some work.
Really really. Let's do something together.'

Even though he has no kids, he looks like someone's dad.
You know the type;
kind around the eyes,
lived-in body. You make up songs and sing them. Peter is
lovely.
Takes you out for food most days. Buys you chicken and
chips
listens when you complain about
English combined
performing arts and psychology
buys you Malibu and Coke
or Bacardi and Coke
or Martini and lemonade. You take a detour one night
after the studio
in the back of Peter's car.
The next day
you are talking to your mum in your bedroom.
Watch her pick up the dress you were wearing,
the red shirt dress
now streaky in the inside back,
unicorn silver. Magic.
You see her throw it back down on the bed.
'What's all that?' she is saying
'What's all what?' you are saying
You're terrified, but you don't dare show it.
You're relieved when she changes the subject.

And all because of some fumble in the car,
some emission
some almost-sex
All because of some nonsense you did when you were lonely-
energetic. Full of the stars and full of Malibu and Barcardi and
lemonade and Martini and Coke and all because you couldn't
waste your superpowers by going straight home to bed;
because of these things
Peter is hooked. Wants to start something. Really likes you
(or something). Gazes at you out of the corners of his eyes.

God.

Peter thinks David is a c
u
n
t. And anyone else who knows David is a c
u
n
t,
well. They get you.
Peter says he loves you. Says he really thinks he loves you. Ah
well, good. Someone has to.
Peter takes you to hotels most of the time (those travel lodges
with the blue and white logos)
in the weekdays to skip college, fuck and drink wine.

17.0

The thing is, says the head booker at the model agency, frowning
we think you're stunning. Obviously, we think you're stunning. B u t
you're very busty for fashion. You could try to drop a few pounds. We'd love to put you in our commercial division but your look might be too strong for that. It's Manchester, y'know? London is a stronger market, but you'd really have to be living there. And they're very strict on measurements down there, but we could try to help you. In any case, it's not easy for Black Girls. If they have another one on their books, they're not going to take you. I'm just being honest, y'know?
She is tossing her bobbed blonde hair around and saying all of these things as if they weren't important. As if it isn't my whole life she's talking about. I have to get out of this town. I need my life to be different, need a career. I need to be away from Grandma and Granddad and Mum and David. I can't do anything right. The only person who gets me is Little Roo. Mum and David are always fighting. I need a way out; some solid escape. I watch fashion TV all day every day. The models are dewy and long and skinny and gleaming. I try everything to shrink. I drink Diet Coke and take bread off my sandwiches and eat Jamaican Water Crackers instead of food. I hear that chewing gum tricks your body into thinking that you're eating, so I buy sugar-free gum every chance I get. I do the New York City Ballet training video every day without fail. Even when I'm cold all the time and always want to sleep, I

still have the deep arch in my back and my boobs are going
nowhere. Try not to wiggle your bum when you walk, say the
girls at the agency. You're modelling the clothes, not your body.
Peter says they don't know what they're talking about.
He knows a man who knows a man in the next town. Soon,
I'm doing trade shows for small clothing brands and local
catalogue shoots.
Mum looks like I've punched her in the face when I refuse to
apply for university. What's the point? I say. I sing. I dance.
I'm an actress and a model, now. I can do it all without school.
What I do well, you can't go to school for, Mum. I realize
how that sounds but I don't care. It's already isolating being at
sixth-form college, not able to relate to anyone else because I'm
with Peter, a grown man their dads' age. A man who doesn't
like it if I go out, unless I'm with him. I feel large and black
and old before my time. Nobody else who is seventeen looks
my way. I'm not tiny or light enough, and my hair is doing
weird things. I can't talk to anyone about Peter. It is a secret
with sharp edges,
a thick serrated weight.
Mum pretends she doesn't know a thing. She knows,
I know she knows. Marcia knows I know she knows;
she skirts around the subject once or twice. We do a pretty
dance.

'I hope you're making decisions that won't affect your life,' she is saying.

'Do you have a boyfriend yet?' she is asking.

David is delighted at the tension in the house. He can be horrible to me and nice to mum, or the other way around, at his leisure.

'Get an education. Your looks will only get you so far, lady,' he says, getting in my face and

winking,

the fuck.

17.5

Somewhere away down South, near London but not quite
there,
I am singing Whitney Houston covers and wearing
long tight dresses with sparkles that catch the light. Peter
looks after my backing tracks or sometimes we hire a pianist.
My hair is permed and hanging to my shoulders. I look a lot like
Mum used to. Before she was always tired.
College is nearly over. I am almost free. I drink. I drink double
whisky and Coke and Bacardi and Coke and Peter drinks the
best beer they have on draught.

Down South near London,
but not quite there, I am sitting in the pub after the gig with
Peter while a naked blonde walks around with an empty pint
glass. The men put pound coins in it.
She's okay, says Peter, but I much prefer the brunette before.
More natural. This one's too skinny and fake boobs aren't my
thing at all.
I know. I say. *I know.*

Up North,
somewhere near home
but far enough away
the music starts and the girl is dancing, the men are leering.
I could do that better, I say.

Yeah but you wouldn't want to be *that,*
says Peter.
Imagine what she must be going through to have to do this. I
mean, what must be running through her head?
She isn't thinking about you, I want to say.
Look at that, Peter says, sneering. The corner of his mouth is
twisted up.
I can see everything, he says,
even the pink.
You paid for it, I say,
you're part of it. So why complain?
Let's not argue again, says Peter, glaring at me. It's the worst
he's ever looked.

Later, after the sex, when he shows me the film he made of it, I
can't look. It's like watching someone punch me, again and
again, in the stomach.
I have learned that I put myself in another place sometimes. Is
that where the girls go when they dance in that awful pub? I
hope I see them in another dimension sometime. We can chat
about the animals. There are far too many of them to us
and mostly, they rule the world.

18.0

David and Mum
fight then make up
fight then make up again.
Little Roo starts a chess club at high school.
He is razor sharp and almost fourteen
beats everyone, even adults. He'll have your queen while you're
still trying to protect your little pieces. He has an analytical
and creative brain, says Peter. He could go far, if he wanted.
Peter tells you he wants to be with you every day.
Peter
phones you up six times while you're out shopping to 'see how
you are'
Peter seems to think he's protecting
you from the world, and men.
Peter says you flirt too much,
reel it in.
David suspects
something. David is angry. Says
'Is there something I ought to be jealous about?'
in that creepy way of his.
Mum sees everything, asks nothing. Carries on going to work
and coming home and sleeping and going to work and coming
home and not getting enough sleep. David keeps sweet things
locked up in drawers,

Chocolate-chip muffins, biscuits, Jammie Dodgers, rows and
rows of Jaffa Cakes.
And will not let anybody at them. He acts more and more
bizarrely,
buying comics, cakes and CDs and more cakes
on Marcia's credit card. Hundreds and hundreds of
pounds' worth of shit
locked up in cupboards.

You
reduce food to 1200 calories
reduce food to 1000 calories
don't tell anyone what's happening with Peter
He wants to get engaged. Oh God.
He says, 'You're losing too much weight.
Eat. Please eat.'
But your hipbones feel more real than anything
two trophies
flanking you, holding you upright
telling you thank you thank you; we love your hard work
and anyway,
you're sorry for Peter
but you want out.
You need something, but you don't know what.

You find that there are internet sites you can
go to and chat with other frustrated people
in the world.
Peter says, 'You can do all that, but only if I'm involved.'

From lycos.com
you meet
AISHA who is tall,
Persian
long haired
so beautiful you can barely stand to look at her.
'That's your boyfriend?' she says, gesturing towards Peter. You nod,
but you don't want it to be true.

You write a book
about four middle-class white women
with long shiny hair and ordinary families
dealing with marital and career problems
and mild lesbianism.
You call it *Swinging Roundabouts*, and all the publishers say,
'Good effort, but it's not what we're looking for.'

You write songs
record them
nothing works
nothing works
You're probably a lesbian.
You think about women
all the time. ALL OF THE TIME.

From alt.com

you meet

CARYN

'You know, I'm going to castrate him,' she says of her boyfriend (who is waiting for her in a minian in the car park outside).

'Yeah, it's all arranged. He doesn't mind. We're working our way up to it.'

You laugh. But her face is straight.

'No, I'm serious,' she says. 'Absolutely serious. We've been planning this for a really long time. There are lots of people doing the same, online and stuff. It's a thing we're doing to illustrate my complete control in the relationship and Martin's submission. I can't wait. It's going to be really exciting for us. A kind of pinnacle. It will vastly improve our dynamic, you know?'

'We'd love you to join us,' she says. 'Have some fun one night. Martin doesn't need to watch or participate. He can listen from another room, if you'd prefer. That'd mess with his head

haha

He'd be into that.'

Oh, I got you this, she says, getting a package out of her rucksack.

You open it. It's a toe ring.

The next time you speak online, she says

'I'm in love with you. Really, I am.'

You move in with Peter.
Marcia comes round to visit and sighs a lot,
saying nothing at all to you except
'Grandma and Granddad think you're ruining your life,'
and
'David's a pain in the arse'
and
'it's nice what you've done with the place, it's so tidy.'
You clean your new house from top to bottom, often.
You remember Linford's kitchen floor and shudder. You make
your own rules and you have your own house
things can be exactly as you want. No red home. No terrible
teeth. No oily moustaches. Just you and disinfectant and
counting calories and fucking. Just you and cleaning, and
household bleach,
and Peter.

And all you can do is break.

break.
Tell Peter you're leaving
one night when he comes home drunk.
He slams the door, nearly taking it off its hinges. You move out.

THREE

Roo can play any instrument you give him,
gifted like that. Pure talent. Loves to drum but can't sit still at
school. Lacks focus.
Isn't checked in, they say. Fell in with bad company, they say.
or perhaps he is the bad company, they say
either way it needs to stop.

Mum calls. Roo stopped his piano lessons to go and hang out on street corners.
Says Mum,
'I can smell it on him. The outside.'

Mum calls. Mum says Roo put a hole in the living-room door with a cricket bat.

Mum is nearly crying. 'It's drugs, I think,' she says.

'It's messing him up. He's changing. He's not going to school anymore.'

Mum calls.
'A GUN,'
she says
'I just threw a 9mm in the bin!
Come and get your brother. I swear I'm going to kill him or
kick him out.
I can't do this. I'm exhausted. I don't feel well at all.'
Instead you
head to Manchester,
which is delightful and grim,
move into a bedsit in Salford. Fifty pounds a week, shared
bathroom.
Drink a bottle of red most days. Hear through the vine that
Peter's divorce came through three months after you left
and he is drinking his days away

Love
Manchester. By day
temp in an office in a glass-fronted tower
by night
go out, on the pills.

the ninety-eight blues

It's a coldasfuck night out there
and there are *no stars in the sky as far as you can see*
but that's no problem, you can make your own. There is a track
in the house charts with those exact words. You'll be dancing
to it later. You smile at your reflection in the long wall mirror
mounted behind your door. Tonight you are kitted out from
top to toe in brand-new clothes,
    a short figure-hugging purple dress
    and black high heels. The person staring back at you looks
pretty good. If you weren't her you might very well want to be.
As you switch off the TV your stomach is nervous. You lock
up, go down the dreadful pink corridor and brown-carpeted
stairs out into the night. You live at the nicer end of Salford.
The higher end, near the football grounds, just before Salford
becomes Prestwich, where the mock-Tudor houses mark the
end of the street.
    There's a thin layer of new ice on the ground, so you'll want
to be treading carefully on those heels. Your breath forms
wispy tendrils in the dark blue air. The double decker bus
that runs through Salford comes in less than fifteen minutes,
a godsend in weather like this. Still singing away to yourself,
you climb to the top row of the bus to view the streets from up
above. It's one straight road into Manchester city centre, past
the school fields and the high-rise estates at either side. There's
always some violent dispute going on between the groups from
both estates, the inhabitants of which proudly hail from one
tower or the other. It's never out of the newspaper. All that

separates the two towers is the main road, the newsagent's, the bookies and two high strips of barbed wire at either side.

After you pass the museum
and the Apollo concert hall
across from the parklands of icy grass, the new police station and the vacant lots, another bus pulls up at the lights beside yours
and a boy who is sitting with his friends on the top tier blows you a kiss. You wipe away the condensation with a gloved finger so you can see him more clearly. You give them all a wave.

You start to come up
you start to roll
about two minutes from the town centre by Deansgate Locks.

You feel the rush inside, the
stirrings
the hot joy drips
things soften in focus.

You need something to chew.

Leaning forward, you pop some strawberry gum loudly in your mouth and ask the man on the double seat opposite you if he doesn't think the overhead view of the coloured lights reflected in the water isn't one of the most beautiful things that he has ever seen. He doesn't reply. The lady beside you pretends she hasn't heard you either. You don't care. You're starting to feel

superstar brilliant.

By the time you reach the locks and you get into the bar, your new friend Paulette is already there. After all, this is her local, the very place where the two of you met, just two months ago. Every single time you're here the music gets better.

You are electric. Your head is swimming
you sweat
the beat reaches your bones.
You stir
from your head to your fingertips,
you can feel it.
You can feel it in your heels,
even the soles of your feet are happy. You can't see your other
friends
but feel sure they must be safe;
you'll see them soon enough. The place is full of people
waiting to be discovered.
When you connect with everyone again it is time to get into
the club. Paulette is laughing at you
because you clearly dropped a pill already.
'Let's do another,' she says. 'While it's empty in here.'
The beat is like a pulse;
everything inside you is liquid precious. There is so much to
say. You tell Paulette how much you love her and that things
will work out fine with the divorce and custody of her little
boy. She's giggling,
she says you're off your head. You can't argue with that. You
find your new friend Carl talking to a group of people. You
kiss him. You two don't like each other like that at all, not
really, but tonight
but tonight
his tongue tastes of bourbon and Coke
It's a heady stomach, this euphoria. You laugh at each other.
His face is contorting and yours must be too, because you
can feel the front row of your teeth clamping down onto your
lower lip. It's going to hurt tomorrow. People around you are
gyrating to

'We can make our own stars.' To the left of you, Paulette is dancing in a pool of light.

You want to call Roo and tell him

Pack up your things and move to Manchester. Away from Mum and David. Let's share a bedsit and write films or something. Something like that.

Mid-conversation with a stranger, you forget, momentarily, what exactly it is that they are talking about.

Sorry what's that you were saying?

and then they laugh and say,

You were talking, not me.

This happens. It does.

This happens, you say. *Oh, it happens. Sometimes but not often. Or not always, but often.*

Shit, they say. *You sound like a poem.*

What drugs are you on tonight, poet?

It is that time already.

Freezing air rushes through the sweatbox

and everyone is making their way out. It is a rude interruption and everyone is worrying about where to go next.

You can't go home high and alone. The people around you decide to continue the party at the place of a friend of a friend of a friend

(tenuous)

but then there is the desperation.

You get the address that somebody has scrawled down on a drinks receipt and most of you make it to the disclosed location.

The after-party is in a new build where the apartments overlook the entire city. It is one of those painfully modern apartments with hardwood flooring, sharp edges and new chrome appliances. The living room is open plan and everything is so white, so sterile, that you wouldn't be at all surprised if there was a bloody operating table or dentist's chair in the middle. You say this out loud but make some slip of the tongue and somebody sniggers. You feel a tiny bit sick but then someone else offers you another, pink and love-heart-shaped. Paulette's favourite pills.

Where is she?

two hours and

you would do anything to stop it getting lighter outside. This time always comes far too soon. Sunday is a horrible thought. Somebody else must be thinking the same thing as you, because he tries to close up the gap in the curtains where a trickle of daylight threatens everything. Things are wearing off and you feel yourself dropping back into the here and now

the terrible here and now

Your new friend gets stuck into a bottle of vodka in the kitchen, so you join him halfheartedly,

but after a quarter of a bottle he rushes home

to pick up his kids from his mother's, he says. What a reason to break up a party.

You,
still drinking and drinking,
feel strangely alert, horribly sober
and no longer recognize anyone. Where did everyone go?

The stereo is pumping out Trance. You can't get into Trance. Not now.

Two people are sitting, awake but motionless. One of them is curled up into a tight ball underneath the dining table. Nobody is taking any notice.

The vodka is keeping you calm. The euphoria has long slipped away. There's a new numb feeling. The heavy. It must be the drink; you can't feel anything much. Still, this is better than what you have been feeling in Real Life recently.

You cry much too often these days.

Example

earlier on in the week when you were walking home from the supermarket with all of your bags and they were cutting into your arm, you suddenly noticed the red of the berries on the holly bushes and became conscious at once that we see the world through filters

and they are all askew

Something Bad Is Here.

People from the party are piling into taxis to go home.

You jump into a car going your way. You're only going as far as the high street.

In the car, nobody speaks. The man who was under the table earlier is sitting in the passenger seat with his head in his hands.

Your throat is dry and the inside of your mouth is tingling, sore.

You can't think straight

but you just have to get on the bus home and soon enough, things will be okay. People are going on with their lives oh so calmly and the futility of it all is killing your head.

This time tomorrow you will already be back into pretending to yourself and everyone else that you're on top of things, standing by the photocopier on the twenty-third floor of the highest glass fronted tower building in Manchester, back to looking down at icy blue air and snow-topped buildings and the busy roads outside,

back to longing to escape. You will be drinking lots of black coffee/brown sugar to try to prevent the slump and wishing time away again.

You tell them

drop me at the lights, I'll bus it from here.

You board the 98

You board the 98 bus

You board the 98 bus shaky

You board the 98 bus shakily and take a seat. A small blonde haired woman climbs and sits ahead of you with two small children. They are making too much noise, it is all too much.

Breathe slow. Breathe slower, but don't over breathe or you're done for. Do not collapse. The lady turns around, gives you a look up and down and draws the children closer to her. You're not sure what she's looking at. Wasn't she young once? At least you're not riding the number 98 judging people.

You could really do with a shower. You hope there's hot water left in the bathroom. You wish you were going home to something or someone instead of an old studio flat with not a lot of light, and a bathroom shared between six. But at fifty pounds a week you get what you pay for.

Don't go under, you say to yourself.

Don't go under.

Just hold it together, you keep saying. And don't look at anyone, or the paranoia will kick in. There is chewing gum on the floor and it's pink and it's fucking disgusting.

There are germs all over the seats, making more of each other. Mating. Think of

something else. Now. Right now. Before the spidery sensation starts on your skin.

Little Roo.

What would Roo be doing now?

You go to call him,

but what useful thing would you say?

You don't call.

When the bus finally arrives at your stop

you think that you can't eat for a long while.

You think that breathing is a little too much effort. You want to pass out, in bed.

You want a drink. You'd like a drink to make the passing smooth.

You shuffle past the Newsagent's, catching a glimpse of your hunched body in the window. Your mouth is sore inside and out. Your lips are cracked and blistered. Your eyes are dark and that thing is happening again. Your face, dripping, all cold mist

wet nose

hot salt.

It is a bitter bright morning, still too much for your eyes. Dull orange car lights. Grey pavement. All of this blue, blue, blue

for as far as you can see and no sun in the sky.

gamma hydroxybluthate

I wake up on someone's
sofa. Paulette is smiling
down at me, playing with
her blonde highlighted posh
Manchester hair.

How cute. She's awake.
Oh, how cute.

I wake up on someone's
sofa. Paulette is smiling
down at me, playing with
her blonde highlighted posh
Manchester hair.

SO much happened while
you were asleep, she says.
SOOOOOO much. But I
don't want to talk about it
right now. Tell you when we
leave. Tell you everything.

I wake up on someone's
sofa. Paulette is smiling
down at me, playing with her
shiny blonde highlighted
posh Manchester hair.

Did I just wake up?
I ask, wide-eyed.
Paulette is laughing at my
word choices.
'I think you mean . . .
have I been knocked out
for this long? Yes you have,
sleepy head!'

I wake up on someone's
sofa. Paulette is smiling
down at me, playing with her
shiny feathered highlighted
posh Manchester hair.

I have been out clean for
over 8 hours and she's
high as a blimp. We have
discovered GHB, the liquid
party drug that smells like
chemicals and tastes worse.
It's clear, like
water,
and makes you feel
amazing . . . high and drunk
at the same time. But a sip
too much and you're out for
the count. For hours.

'Shit went down last night,' she says. 'You passed out and missed it all!

How much G did they give you?'

'A capful,' I tell her. 'The vodka bottle capful.'

'Shit, man,' she says, hands over her eyes.

'That's how they fucked up. That was a big vodka bottle. A super large dose. You're supposed to measure one of the regular sized capfuls. Are you feeling okay?'

I climb to my feet, wobbling somewhat

'Fine.'

'Kid,' she laughs, 'you have *angels*.'

We get in the car and drive.

'So *what* happened when I was asleep? What did you lot get up to?'

'Ah,' she says. 'Things got a bit too wild for me actually.'

The colour in her face has changed. Her eyes are dark, looking the other way.

I suddenly want to hug her but I do not dare.

'Be careful,' she says, 'not to drink any of these water bottles in the back here. I don't know what's what.'

'Where's my kitbag?' I croak.

Paulette passes me our drug survival kit, which includes Lucozade pills, plasters, Bonjela (for the mouth ulcers), orange juice for vitamin C,

and a melted Easter egg for sugar and energy. We share the chocolate on the way.

I love Paulette. She has ten years on me and a frightening temper, but she's my best friend for now. It's nice to have a woman in my life. I'd totally kiss her, but she's straight as an arrow.

We both like powder and we both love pills and attention but my favourite days with her are those when we're with her little boy

feeding ducks
looking out at the water. Pillheads love stillness as much as
anyone.

Two weeks later,
we are eating a curry with the little one,
watching a documentary on a man with psychosis
and he is talking about how, one morning while high on
GHB,
something told him to knock all of his teeth out with a
hammer. So he did.
I shudder.
Paulette hugs her kid close into her and says, to me
'Some people are just so self-destructive. God.'
'Terrible,' I say.
'Terrible,' she says.

19.8

Gemma from the agency: You know what this is, right?

Me: Yes I do.

Paulette: [Having more trouble with this than me] Yes.

Gemma from the agency: [Looking at me] This isn't a model agency. I just say this because you're still very young and you must be informed, you see; I have to cover my back . . .

Me: Yeah, I know what this is. I'm fine with it.

Gemma from the agency: Because some girls think that it's just dates and functions, and it's really not. This is the sex industry.

Me: That's fine.

[Gemma excuses herself, takes a call. Returns.]

Gemma from the agency: There's a party happening in a penthouse at xxxxxxxxxx and the client loves the sound of you. It'll be lovely. Top Notch people. You want to go? You look stunning as you are.

Me: Yes, I'll go.

Gemma from the agency: Okay, great! [Turns to Paulette] I'll find something for you later, hopefully.

Mr Jumeriah at the Penthouse.

I arrive at the penthouse. A lady dressed in a trouser suit is
sitting at a reception desk, like we're at the office or something.
Go straight through and say hello to him, she smiles.
I pass through the annex to get to the master bedroom,
approaching a table with powder like cocaine,
foil and glass bottles on it.
What's all this? I whisper to myself.
Oh, says his PA, coming up behind me
'It's crack. But don't worry, it's totally optional,
hahaha.'
I am soon to learn that this is standard practice for Mr
Jumeriah, who is walking around in the other room in his
boxers, making incoherent noises. He beckons me with a nod
through the frame of a doorway. There, sitting on the bed, are
two girls in swimsuits, sipping wine.
'Hey!' they say. 'He just wants you to dance, really . . .
there are some bikinis in the basket. Pick one, any one.
Oh my God, that white would look good on you.
Oh my God, gorgeous skin, so jealous.
Oh my God, is that your real hair or extensions?'
Afterwards, I am ushered to another room, where six girls in
bikinis are sitting with cups of milky tea
biscuits
eclairs
crisps and cupcakes
we talk about make-up, *X Factor*, the news and the fact that
we'd never seen anyone on crack before

and isn't it great that we didn't even need to get naked this time, let alone touch him? Mr Jumeriah is a legend around these parts. Apparently he likes to dance in hotel rooms with young women, and that's about it.

Afterwards, the PA pays us each some money in an envelope, and everyone goes home. On the way home I call Roo and ask him what drugs he's tried.

'Ah, it's nothing,' he says. 'I'm not really into it. Just a bit of weed. Sometimes something else, you know, but no big deal. No hard stuff. No H or crack or nothing.'

20.0

On the week of my birthday I go to Chorley to visit my
mum for a couple of days. I have a dry, scratchy throat and
am experiencing visual trails when I move too fast and a
permanent sense of being off-balance, which is normal by now.
All the floors are moving, always. I feel heavier than normal.
And my breathing is off.

It is a cold day and the tips of my fingers are white. The
circulation in my extremities is worse than usual. Mum and
I go to the bank. Her eyes are unnaturally bright and she is
talking about a holiday she wants to take. She is shivering a
little and there is something chattery and fragile about her. I
want to hold her hands

but I can't feel my own. A daughter with no warmth in her
body.

'Malta . . . or Tenerife,'

Mum is saying,

'both good places to relax.'

She seems different, somehow

and

her voice seems to be coming to me from far away.

I say,

'Mum

something is weird. I feel shak—

I feel shaky.'

The next thing I know, I'm on the floor and the bank people
are giving me water.

'You passed out,'
someone says.
'You alright, love?'
how ya feeling?
Later on that night I am lying in bed
and the shadows are terrifying me. It feels as though the
ceiling is coming down to meet the floor. Then a dark hooded
figure runs towards me and back through the doorway.
    Someone is out to get me,
I just know it. There is pressure at the back of my head.
My teeth are getting in the way.
I can't get the words out.
Sweating, I get to my feet and stagger to Mum's room
I try to scream,
but my voice is caught in its box and falls out ragged,
'Mum!
Mum!
Someone's trying to get me. I'm unwell.'
Mum sits up at once in bed.
'NO,' she screams back
'No, you are not. You are EXHAUSTED! And coming down
from whatever it is you've been on.'
    I trudge back to my own bed
but can't sleep
won't sleep.
By the weekend I am back at some after-party with Paulette,
ignoring the sore throat
battling the fever.
'Are you sure', says Paulette. 'You've just been really ill.'
'Fuck it,' I say. 'Let's get back on it.'
It's too late anyway; we're already well away. Paulette and
I have been eating ecstasy tablets like sweets since Friday

afternoon and we are introduced to a group of four men on
Saturday afternoon.

They're in their twenties, and lovely.

Irish Tony,

Dangerous Dave,

Adam and William from Manchester.

We disappear off into the early evening. They call Dave
Dangerous because he has a platinum dye job, and a low drug
threshold. Dangerous Dave gets out of control very quickly.
He's been known to take pisses in bars in full view of everyone
and chuck full pint glasses at people's heads. All the same, I
find him quite lovable and the feeling is mutual.

'You've got really nice features,' says Dangerous.

'Thanks,' I say. 'You got any pills?'

We go to a soulful house event in Blackpool;

we are more young and beautiful than we'll ever be again.

Dangerous and I get high listening to soul music, steal
William's car and go on a joyride

Three hours later and

I might be going under

Tony is in bed with Paulette.

Adam is lost.

Dangerous

is looking for William under the teacups on the draining
board.

'Don't worry about that,' says William.

'It's Ketamine.

Once they drop in the K hole you just have to leave them to it.'

I look up at him. He's a tall, muscular type, but there's something overwhelmingly kind about him.

'What do you want to do?' he asks. 'We could drink some more or just go for a nice breakfast. You've totally fucked the wheels on my car, by the way.'

We choose breakfast and sleep wrapped up in each other for a whole day until we have to get up on Monday for work. Him at the Wellness Centre, me at the office and then out again at night.

We meet again and again
and
as it happens,
we sink into each other.

21.0

'You keep talking about *it*,' says William, 'but I don't know what *it* is. You're making me think scary things.'

We are doing the moves again, that dance of near-truth. I'm exhausted. And I don't know what else to say.

'Scary things like what?'

'You tell me,' he says, although I'm sure he doesn't need me to.

And then I think,

There's nothing for it. This is probably a waste of my time anyway.

So to end it all, I say,

'Escort. Party girl. Whatever you want to call it. Alright? Good. Well, now you know. Good.'

He says,

'Right.'

I say

'So move on if you wish, now you know everything. This has been fun

or whatever. It is what it is. Cool.'

He looks at me like I hit him in the face.

'Don't be silly. I love you, you idiot.'

We continue drinking beer, shooting pool. My heart is overthrown, but I play it down.

on the monday

Paulette says I never should have told him. Never ever.
Just wait, says she.
He'll only throw it in your face. Yeah, he'll use it against
you.
Just wait, says she. He'll be out the door.

He isn't. He stays.
I can hardly believe it. It feels like the bottom will drop out
of our thing.
Any
Moment
Now. When he sleeps, his arm wrapped around me, I stare at
his eyelashes in the dark and hope he never leaves. Sometimes I
hold my breath to give the thing some weight. Some promise.

Paulette gets drunk one night, phones me up and calls me
some names.
I never see her again.

RE
CREATION.

If, God forbid, anything should happen to you
(I hold my breath every time you leave the house
for a good twenty seconds
so it does not
but if it does),
  if it does and someone (anyone) asks me what first struck
me about you, remember, I would say your face. The openness
of your face, your kind eyes. Large enough to see the
wholewideworld. And your thick hands, and your gentleness.
Those are some solid things to remember about a person. You
are a strapping Taurus and you know how to stay.

I don't know what is in the pills I took tonight
but I am seeing things. The map, the entire
map of the world as I know it is appearing
across your skin. All the Africas of the
universe stretched across your taut skin. The
golden globe of the planet,
your pores, the hairs on your arms, a city each.
Should I call, say,
Should I call and ask Mum, Why?
Should I tell Little Roo we love him? You say
no, not right now. Or you take my hand and
say
See how you feel tomorrow. They're going to know you're on
something. No phone calls for now.

21.2

Mum is in the house alone a lot.
She organizes things, paints her nails orange
or in purple glitter
and is mostly lonely. Roo likes to roam the streets at night.
David is seeing some woman in the next town. A woman
with no teeth.
says Mum, matter of factly.

                              CA said Mum, matter of factly.
                     CA (she likes to use hospital abbreviations)
                 Of course CA, I think to myself. Of course CA.
                                      I could feel it coming.

This is how we came to know: She called me into the room.
She called, 'Come and feel this for me baby and tell me.'
So I did. It was hard. Pebble-sized.
We didn't take any chances. I made the call and she was in
and they took a biopsy
and it's
CA,
of fucking course.

David is asking me if I know what it means,
Of course I fucking know. I dreamed it. I dreamed it up.

Roo doesn't really undertand it
Is nodding but it isn't going in;
or maybe it is. You wouldn't know.
He has a strong back and arms now
and sinews and hair sprouting
all over his face. He got contact lenses in too these days.
His eyes are often pink.

Mum loses a breast. Gains another, round and full.
Silicone. Goes to Malta for a holiday
Her limbs swell
lymphoedema, they say.
William massages her sometimes
when we visit,
not I.
I think (and feel like a rat). I look at her
look away
and wonder
how
why
why
and how.

And then . . .
Remission they say.
Remission. She's stronger.
We feel like a family. Things might be improving.
William and I visit more these days, because David is off
fucking the toothless woman.
I tell her what's happening with me,
and things are really changing. I dropped the night work,
kept the day work
got an acting agent
and a job interview
booked a modelling job
and my poems are being published in a literary magazine.
Samson is visiting more often these days. He stays and talks
to Mum about her life. About what's happening in *his* life
these days. He's married again now. Loved up with a lady he
met on the army barracks. Mum listens and listens and looks
out of the windows and smiles.
William rubs her arms and legs. Lets the lymph nodes drain,
or something
not I.
I think (and feel like a rat). I look at her
look away and wonder
how
why
why
and how.

Grandma and Granddad think the house is a disgrace
but say less these days. Roo lives with Mum and does all her
shopping and picks up her bits
but cannot keep the house well.

Not one of us can play house well.

RE
(2)   CREATION.

There is something underneath my seams. What's new?

It is morning. We make a hamper of iced buns that we bought from the deli and sparkling wine to take to the park. We bathe in green open spaces as often as we can and take Polaroid pictures and hold hands, wondering how we found each other. Shuddering at the idea that it might never have happened. Sometimes the facts around our first meetings change. Sometimes Paulette was there; other times she wasn't. Sometimes she was in bed with Irish Tony and sometimes it was Adam. But the facts remained, he stared up at me and the air was warm and whistling

and we left them all to start something else.

There is something underneath my seams,

but it's a given. Furthermore I don't care. It's a still, cool day in Manchester. The air smells like grass and trees and we are making our way up a large, large hill.

I came here as a child, he says. It's my favourite park in the world. I want to laugh because I don't know that he's travelled all that much. But a favourite park is a favourite park; and this is as good as any other. The stately home gleams in the distance and I wonder. How I could be so entirely lucky.

Just a little further now, he is saying, shivering in a cream polo-neck. I have on his coat. Our fingers are interlocked like stars, like a fixed shape.

Just up here, he says, and we turn the corner to continue up the hill. I turn to ask how far now and he has dropped to his knee, his face an open book.

I say yes without pausing (I have already said yes).
But I won't lie . . .

still there are some small sharp things in the lining of my heart. Some things like animals stalking my body. Animals inside.

22.2

William and I are woken up by the police on the phone.
Roo has been arrested
(again). He's sitting in Preston in custody. He's been robbing
people in the area, they say. Snatching their phones, bank cards,
drugs, handbags
at knifepoint. I may need to go down to the station, they say.
He's in a bit of bother.

They release him later on in the day.
No charge.

'Handbags? Lies. I'd never rob a woman.'
he says in the back of the car.

These days I go easy on the drugs. A couple of pills over the weekends, if that. I have a job at an insolvency practice, manning the phones on the front desk and ordering office supplies.

William is a managing director at a health club in Manchester.
just got promoted. We go to the theatre often and I write poems about life and how sticky everything is

but still things are Not Right

Some days I have to breathe into paper bags. I'm getting light-headed, often.

Some days I can't lift my head off the pillow. A lot of days I cool-sweat.

I say,

We need to go down South. I need to Get Away. I'm going crazy here. The flat is too square and the ceilings too low. I'm too close to everyone and always, always too far. What can I do for Little Roo when I cannot do anything, not anything for myself?

There is not enough light, I say,

twisting my engagement ring on my finger.

you see it and see it but you never really see it

That thing that you don't want to happen happens, happens anyway,
    remember?

She says, again,
'Baby, come and feel this for me.'
And I don't want to. Because I know, I really do. Secretly
we all know the bad things that are about to happen. It's
already inside us, some coding in the body. Already behind the
curtain, glowing red. Already dreamed, And it comes
    and it goes
    and it comes again

                                                        CA
                                          of fucking course.

Ah, the ticking time bomb of a body. You try to live life.
And work for your children and hustle and sweat and fuck and
work and call out for love and cry for love and have
children and work and study and sleep in bed and save and
worry about your bleeding gums
    and you still go, in the end.

She was beautiful.
We dressed her in purple and white.

William and I made the drive up from London and were the
last to arrive. When we got to the hospice, there were many old
and familiar faces. Samson was there with his wife.

Linford's face had ballooned over the years.

Hi
said Linford

How are you,
said Linford.

I hope you people are
doing okay, said
Linford.

You look well. Still
modelling?
said Linford,
completely beside himself.

Grandma and Granddad were wonderfully stoic. Asked me
how work was going. Handed out sandwiches and plastic cups
of cornmeal porridge. Little Roo collapsed in my arms. The
only normal reaction around.

As for me, I couldn't feel a thing.

My mum's brother brought in some KFC. We all sat around the body speaking politely about how we were getting on. I did all of the calls, to the registrar of births and deaths and the undertaker. Little Roo sat motionless in a chair in the waiting room.

The next day we all sat at my mum's house and William and I made everyone cups of tea while we discussed the funeral arrangements. An uncle's girlfriend (an Englishwoman) suggested a cold finger buffet for the funeral reception and Granddad interjected right away

'Nah man, black people don't eat cold food.'

She is beautiful.
We burn her body in purple and white
with red nails.

The funeral is a handful of errors, for a variety of reasons.

1. Marcia is late as usual (the undertakers' fault, of course, not hers).
2. They open the casket at the wrong time and the shock of seeing Marcia's empty body; the shell of her before I am prepared causes me to burst at once into hysterical laughter.
3. Terence turns up, looking devastated.
4. Linford turns up, looking pale and bloated and withdrawn.
5. They both keep their distance.
6. David is nowhere to be seen.
7. Grandma outdoes herself on the food. The rice and peas. To die for. Ha.

Am I dreaming? No. No red uniform. No failing light switch.

I alternate between Jack Daniel's and Jameson the following week or so to deal with the shock.

Little Roo is almost eighteen and will not talk.

an end

What is the difference between the beginning and the end?
I stare hard at my hands and do not recognize them. I take off
the diamond to wash up the plates
    and won't or can't put the thing back on.

One week later,
                the ring was – is – still
                              on the kitchen sink. What's
the difference between love and the end? There isn't a
difference, is there? William asked about the ring again and I
said
'It's on the sink, where I left it.'
        He saw it in my face; I saw it in his. William watched
me slink away.

                        William watches me slink away.

You haven't put your ring back on for a while,
                      says William,
a week after that.

No, I haven't, I say. Not yet. I just . . .

I just . . .

And we stand there

seeing each other for the first time

not crying about it. Neither one of us is dead. It's just time to
move on, I figure.

And so,

that week ends and another week starts and it looks like I'm
moving out. No more fixed shape. I can only see things in fits
and starts. In pieces. I cannot have a family; freedom is all I
need.

I need to be free to catch up with myself.

Wishes do come true; my new street in London looks fresh out of a picture book. Like something Roo and I would have drawn. Some scene that would have given me cause to consult the powder-blue book of magic, that I could have wishedmyself right into. I am in the middle of Primrose Hill, surrounded by candy-coloured houses and Russian resaurants and blonde curly-haired children and nannies and gourmet cafés and hot yoga studios everywhere. Money everywhere. Even the sky looks expensive. I live in a bedsit on the top floor of one of the houses. Life is all around.

Inside, though, I hardly feel a thing. William is never off the phone asking me again and again if I need anything. I say no, no and no,

and stop picking up his calls. These days all I do is lie on the old daybed at the top of the house, staring hard at the white popcorn ceiling.

heaven 1

(i) Our mother is dead
certainly gone.
Everything of her is scattered energy
and, if the Bible is to believed, she is back to her own
beginning.
Dust.

(ii) Everyone else stayed up in the North, ageing.
I'm far enough away to forget, except during sleep. I live
in London, where the hours are shorter, where the days in a
month are fewer.

(iii) Roo is up North,
always between one town and the next. Half at Mum's
house
half somewhere else. Grandma can never get hold of him,
he's not an easy one to pin down. He changes his number
about three times a month and sells anything you want. He
stores the things at Mum's house, I hear.
Good stuff too, I hear
But he's not so talkative. Wears a lot of dark clothes. Likes to
cover up his face a lot. If you phone him you have to push for a
conversation
and, since neither of us are strong in that
not much gets said.

We stick with the usuals
Me: Have you spoken to Grandma and Granddad?
Him: Nah.
Me: You should call them.
Him: You spoke to them?
Me: Yeah, last month.
Him: . . .
Me: Have you spoken to Samson.
Him: No.
Etc., etc., etc.

One night on the phone,
Roo says he saw Sonny in KFC and Sonny tried to blank
him. Just walked past, like he wasn't even there. He says
something about someone punching a wall but the phone line
keeps cutting.
'Wait,
who tried to punch a wall?' I ask, for clarity.
Roo makes a noise in his throat
and the line goes dead.
When I go on his Facebook page, he's posing with a bottle of
Cîroc in one hand, a bottle of Hennessy in the other,
with a bandage around that hand,
which answers the question.

(iv) I take the train up North.
Roo has a wild beard. His hairline is farther back than I
remember.
'How's William?'
he says, after a while

'Ah, it just didn't work out,'
I say.
I don't say . . .
I left William in the worst possible way. Two weeks after the funeral.
I don't say . . .
all I see is pitch grey. I'm under
I don't say . . .
I don't feel like a real person
I'm damn near numb, mostly.
Instead I say,
It just wasn't working, you know.
Roo stubs out his cigarette. A look passes across his face but I don't know what it is.

(v) We go out for the evening. I drink eight vodkas on the Rocks and start to feel again.
I think my brother is the most beautiful person I've ever met.
The owner of the pub comes over
stares at my chest
and tells us Roo is not allowed here
on account of the crimes.
I say, 'Give him a break. We just lost our mum.'
He says,
'Yeah, I read it in the paper, God rest her soul. But my hands are tied and it's a police matter now. You look sexy tonight, though, luv. As always, as always.'
I down a tequila shot for the road and say,
'Thanks for nothing, dickhead.'

(vi) In the morning
I get the train back to London
leaving Roo with Marcia's ashes. It's time to find
some kind of night work again.

FOUR

twelve minutes past one

It is a tragic riot, the way that things circle. You could kill yourself laughing, I tell you.

I am thinking of the soft afternoons when I would watch cricket indoors with Granddad during the summer holidays. It was the only sport he was into other than snooker, and he always said that you couldn't really call that a sport. Our team was the West Indies, naturally.

Of course, it is some years later now, and there is a cricketer standing by the bar. He is much older now but still tall, still dashing. I would recognize his face anywhere. O'Connell, his name. He was one of our very favourites. Granddad used to call him brilliant, even though he was white. Always thought he was a man among men to play for a black team. As though he was a big grown man rolling up his trousers, playing in the dirt with children.

And he's in the club. I mean, this is a sick claim to fame, but I'll take it.

It's a dead night tonight. Business is not so good lately. The Eastern European girls have commandeered the only other group of men in here. What can I say? These men like blondes first, brunettes second and then maybe us. There's only me and Angela left. Now I'm very late on rent and Angela's got two kids at home. The air around us is tight and desperate. Angela is dabbing perfume under her arms to mask it. I like to let them catch the smell.

He has had a drink or two, O'Connell. I go to approach him but this bitch Angela has the same idea. What she lacks in looks she makes up for in everything else. She's pushy as hell. Some men really like that.

O'Connell looks at us, puffs out his chest and says, okay, then, I'm only going to take one of you, so you should both show me what's underneath those dresses. I like to look before I buy. He has a horrible shark grin.

I am stifling a smile. We all know who's going to win this one. If I've got anything, it's nice tits. A good face and nice tits. Angela is skinnier than me, older by nearly ten years, and she's had the kids. Plus, she has that hardness in the face, like she can't really do this anymore. I thought that she'd give up now but she's going for it.

They put some Sade track on – 'Jezebel', which is a joke. They are cheesy in the West End.

I take down my straps and pull down the front of my dress, letting it hang at the waist. He smiles at me. He winks. Angela does exactly the same and his smile sort of freezes on his face. And I hope he isn't going to ask for both of us after all, because I can't be sharing my money. He looks at her for such a long time that it gets uncomfortable, even for me. The corner of his lip turns up and he mouths the word 'fuck'. Then he starts to laugh, because she's seen better days and the other people in the club are looking now and so are the girls and the manager and he points at her and says,

Sure you're still in the right job?

She is wearing green contact lenses. Her eyes are glassy. At first I don't know whether they are filling or storming but I can feel electricity in the air, I smell thunder.

She springs up like something wild and goes for him with her nails and her teeth . . .

and he knocks her down.

He leans over her, eyes blazing, a few inches from where her head is and out pours curses upon curses. I can't say them here. I'm thinking, you wouldn't expect this foulness from someone who played for a black team,

and then she's still on the floor holding her face and he kicks her twice.

They call security and the bouncers run over and I can't believe it. Everyone is fawning over him, apologizing; he gets a bottle of champagne on the house. She gets fired. She is holding her ribcage under her breast. There is blood in her mouth as she limps away. But it isn't my business, I repeat to myself. She's nothing to do with me, not really.

Everyone goes back to what they were doing. I go and sit down with O'Connell and his eyes are glazed with a red film and he leans his head back like nothing has happened and says,

Dance

and I do . . .

and in my head I am dancing the lambada, rhumba, merengue

and the polyester curtain that is pulled around us is made of silk and his hands are the applause . . . hard, strong, everywhere

and my sweat smell is the night air in the tropics – the beach and the sand and the yellow moon.

I am suddenly more tired than I've ever been but I'm a professional, so I keep on dancing, you know, even though he is not a man among men at all.

I am spinning, smiling, sinking. All of the waves in me are crashing
while upstairs, at the same time, Angela is crossing the road. This is where everything hardens.

I am still downstairs preparing to take more of O'Connell's money because the bastard can't get enough,
he is foaming at the mouth.

Later, the doorman is sitting on the step, whiter than usual. He says Angela just stepped into the road looking right at the oncoming traffic like she meant to get hurt.
He says she didn't look good. She didn't look good at all.
That is when I realize that she might as well be family. There is a wound in my chest, harder than a cricket ball.

I go back downstairs. The cricketer wants another dance. Sade plays again; I hear my heart in my ears.
Of course I keep on dancing. Time is money.

heaven 1.5

I look in the mirror one night;
the moon is too thick. And I see other things.
I look in the mirror.
I cut off a lot of my hair tonight.
A red wine decision. Red home, red house, red, red wine.
I bind up my chest. I breathe out. Better.

heaven 2

The person I take home tonight smells perfumy. Like nothing bad but nothing particularly good. Also, they have plenty of wispy, long hair. It's all very upsetting.

We met tonight in a club called Heaven. I sank two cheapish bottles of red before I left the house. Easy, easy, and warm, warm.

My two going-out friends, as usual, were not drinking half as much as I, or nearly as fast. I can't imagine socializing sober. They are from a different planet, perfectly content to be out without liquid protection. Last night I couldn't hold a conversation with either one of them because my eyes were darting around the room, dizzy, searching for the brightest distraction. They rolled their eyes at me (they are forever rolling their eyes) and told me to take it easy. Slow it down, they said.

I thought
What the fuck for? We're young only once
and it's easy for you both to say. My world needs cushions.
I kissed someone
because they said I smelled good
they said I was beautiful
the walls were getting tighter
and it was too hot and dark and full of strangers and I wanted to feel something. Red wine

a hot prayer,
was making me feel deliciously larger than myself. You can
always rely on wine.

There was nothing stopping me, as always. I was free. My
friends left. I went back with the stranger

the usual story (I hate it and hate it but can't face myself
alone some mornings) This person was talking at me all the
while about how they don't normally do this.

I thought, please just be quiet,
and kept on my T-shirt and socks.

also

Marcia visited in my dream just now, saying:

I am sorry. I am definitely sorry.

*I did not die, per se. How would you still be able to talk to me
in your dreams? Can't you see that by now I am entirely fact
and entirely fiction?*

*Pull yourself together. You are an African, the most magical
kind of human there is.*

*I am somewhere else now. I am part human, part metaphysics
and I still haven't worked out which parts of me are which. I love
this new form. I can feel space travelling through me. I am porous
and wondrous and bold.*

and Marcia said

*It's not that I loved to leave,
rather that staying was always completely impossible.*

*You are eighty percent water. Stop getting so wasted. Please.
You should have married the kind one.
This searching, searching for nothing, will kill you.*

Hardly breathing, I go to creep out the door.
'I wish you wouldn't leave,' the stranger says, face down in
the bed. 'I think you're beautiful.'
'I'm sorry, I have to go . . . work,' is all I can manage.
'Nice,' they say. 'Well, you seem in a hurry.'
I must be. I'm already in the street, gone.

The following days are tight, without peace. I buy a fifty-
pound Naomi Campbell-style wig – long, black, with
the fringe, and return to work at the club. I am quietly
wondering about Angela.

Also, I don't have the energy to put up with the men or their requests, or their hands. One of them seems hell-bent on asking about my parents.

'How do you think your mum would feel about you doing this,' asks a *customer*, who no doubt fancies himself a psychiatrist.

'She died two months ago,' I say, deadpan.

'So, my question still stands,' he says.

Fucking smart arse. I grit my teeth; tuck in my claws. When he asks me to dance, I do.

Little Roo

On the phone
our cousin is saying
your brother
tried to end
your brother tried
to end
tried
to
end with a leather black belt
and his girl
stopped him
a belt
a thick
black/brown one
they say
some girl
he was seeing
or maybe
just some girl
stopped him
his room smells like an ashtray
they say
there are cups and plates under his bed
they say
there are holes in the walls in our mum's house. (He can't
keep a house. We cannot keep our houses
no matter how far apart we are
we are bound by fail

failing
hearts failing – we need to sell the house, man.)

They said it was a thick black rope/cable
that Little Roo
sorry
Roo
used around his neck.
I am on the phone.
I can't get hold of him
I down half a bottle of Vodka from the person's fridge and
nearly run out into the night
but whoever I'm with says
you drank too much
come back to bed. There is
nothing you can do from Brixton
I say,
'That's where we are?'
and they look at me.
I try Roo all morning
I get hold of him finally at 12.56 p.m.
and he says

I'm fine now
I get these feelings and they pass. I'm fine now
but I know and he knows
everyone is a long way from FINE. Roo says
last week I decided to die
arrogant, but it was my choice to make.
Roo says
remembering everything that has happened
I promptly forgot God's name
Roo says

They say it is a belt
a thick black one
or cable
or whatever. I cannot swallow detail these days.
I go up North. We sit at the doctor's.
I tap my leg in the waiting room. I want to hold Roo's hand
but I don't.
He goes out for a cig and the doctor comes and I say do you
want me to come in with you
and he says

yeah.

And Roo's eyes are glazed
blackshining
and Dr Melling (now grey grey grey
and no longer of interest to me) makes notes
and we're thinking we can't wait this long
to get healed. We're thinking, skin heals.
Why can't we? We're thinking, how long do we have
To travel in blistering rain, exactly? We're thinking,
does life owe us anything. Did we get it wrong? And time is
an animal, man. The years. Time
is killing us
it has us in its teeth
and Dr Melling prints out papers

and says to Roo, 'How long have you been feeling like this?'
Shit. Who can answer a question like that?
We put the papers down (I think we sign them or
something)
  read them, or something
  pick up a prescription, or something
  but I can't be sure;
  I'm under.
And out of nowhere, in the car, Roo says

> *I'm into grime music*
> *these days.*
> *See. An outlet.*
> *Wanna listen?*

He passes me the earphones,
he's good, of course,
 and that's the tragedy. Roo says
> *I'm not taking those fucking antidepressants.*
I don't want to bury you
I say.
He says

> *you won't.*
> *it won't happen again.*

I want to say,
Yes, you're brilliant.
Yes, it hurts. Or
come away with me. But I know he won't.
I say
So, stop living in her house.
The walls are black
the insides are coming away
 it looks like a crack den
let's get this place on the market.
We have to go to Grandma's cos we're right there.

We sit there at Grandma's
we eat her food
he doesn't say much and neither do I
he stares into his potatoes and chicken and macaroni and
cheese.
Grandma's house hasn't changed since he was tiny
sitting in the same chair, eating dinner. Maybe the feelings
haven't changed either.

Finally,
we make our excuses and escape into the night
no one will let us in any of the bars so
we sit in a parking lot across from the precinct.
he smokes a blunt. I drink rum out of the bottle

I'm fucked up.
Where are we? I say

The North of England
he says

unicorns don't exist
I say.

Roo
says
yeah they do
remember the garden?

Things that I could tell you about Little Roo

One. A genius, my little brother.

    Two.   He was playing with his toy cars and tried to close up his throat.

        Three.   His father is a wild, wild huntsman, from a different world.

Four. We rarely talk, but he's my best friend.

true lies

What do you do when all the certainties diametrically oppose each other? When the paradigms can't agree. When the contradictions and horrible info are warring?

Fact. Marcia is beautiful. Fact. Marcia is whole. Fact. Marcia is dead. Fact. Marcia appeared to me as a pregnant Asian girl on the bus clutching her belly and an old Rasta, who smiled at me when he saw that I was reading a book on Jamaica and its politics.

Fact. Roo doesn't care about anyone. Fact. Roo cares too much, about everything. And it's too much for him. Fact. I need to call Roo. He needs to call me. Fact. I hardly do. He never does.

Love / Money

One morning I wake up and understand many things.

Henry Parker is lying beside me making irritating little noises, snoring and grunting and gurgling. I think about covering his head a little with the pillow to drown out the sounds. But it's his bed and his house and I wouldn't want to scare him. It is ten minutes to six and I can't get back to sleep. We are south of London, in Surrey, in his lovely low-ceilinged country house with two wings and nine bedrooms. Surrounding the house are two large very well-kept gardens. Henry lives here alone among all of this space and beauty. It is a muggy August morning and the air in the room is still. Well over half of the year has gone by already, which is a worry. I wanted to make something of myself this year. There's still time, I think. Definitely some time.

The bed is large and quite comfortable in theory, with a soft mattress and heavy floral bedspread. It is covered with lots of red and white peonies on a pink background.

The difficulty of being a guest in someone else's house is that you can't just go and get yourself something to eat. I change position to see if that will help. He opens his eyes and says I seem disturbed and I say tell me something I don't know and he chuckles, gurgles and then falls back to sleep. He sleeps with his mouth open. The elderly and babies share similar traits, I notice. Sometimes I am not sure who is taking advantage of whom. I have been here four times now and he always hands me a cream coloured envelope the night before so that he doesn't forget and so things aren't awkward in the morning. An envelope with my name neatly written across it in thick cerulean ink. When we met in person for the first time we discussed our arrangement over sea bass and brandy. I needed the brandy or I wouldn't have had the courage to talk him up a little, because his first proposal was much too low. We were talking about a whole night after all and I agreed on a fee that was lower than I'd like but better than not having the work at all.

Henry was a history lecturer. He hates anything written in the present tense. I wonder what that says about him. Last night we went out for dinner and I had steak for the first time in ages and he had the same. We drank a shot of brandy each. People are always very interested in us, which can become embarrassing because he is short, old and bald.

I think all young people should spend time with somebody much older, although obviously not in these circumstances. Last night in the car we got onto the subject of fatality. He is aware, he said, that he is nearing the end of his life. I, on the other hand, am closer to the beginning of mine. He used the old hill metaphor, which got me to wondering which point exactly I am at on this hill. If I live till I'm eighty, for example, that makes me now just over halfway between the base and the highest peak;

anyway, hills don't have peaks. Mountains do.

I don't think that I'll live a particularly long life. It doesn't bother me.

You gather speed when you're descending.

Henry says he isn't scared of death. It's just as well.

I don't like it when he talks about the kids. We could be getting on alright and then he starts talking about the children, as if I really want to know. There are many pictures dotted around the house. His 'girls' are horsey and plain-looking.

Girls.

His *girls*.

Both of them are at the peak of the mountain and have been supported well and funded throughout their precious lives.

It makes me giggle when I wonder what would happen if the girls found out what their father gets up to in bed with a girl my age. It makes me damn near hysterical, but not because it's funny.

The clock says six o'clock.

Time crawls when you are not having fun.

I do imagine the gravity of what I'm doing. I do consider soul damage. If the very physicality doesn't get you,

it's the paranoia. What would people think?

What would people think of this? What would anybody think?

This catches up with me in the night, or strangles me in the small hours of the morning. I wonder about the outcome of it all. Will I ever be able to tell anyone what I have been? My mind is wandering into dark pockets. I want to jump off the roof.

I open my eyes.

To my surprise he is fully dressed, in a tweed jacket, slacks and green shirt and is shaking me awake. 'You need to wake up,' he is saying, 'my daughter is on her way round to check in on me. And you'd hardly pass for the nurse.'

The clock radio says 9.30 in large red figures.

But Marcia is trying to talk to me. She is trying to talk to me, forever at inopportune times. Deep into the morning and way too early at night. It is often a Wrong Time for the two of us.

I say,

Mum, I can't talk. I'm at work. Tonight maybe?

But there is no point making appointments with her. She comes when she comes when she comes and all I have to do is not test the lightswitches and hope she comes alone.

Marcia says she hasn't met Jesus yet, can you believe it?

Marcia says, play the lottery numbers this week.

Henry is cutting into my thoughts and interrupting Marcia's voice and saying my name again, sounding flustered. Sleepily I climb out of bed and put yesterday's knickers on inside out and then I am putting on my clothes and going down the stairs and taking my bag from the kitchen and he is apologizing profusely, then I am outside and the door is shut behind me.

Henry's large black Doberman, Davies, trots beside me as I make my way down the stony driveway towards the front gate. Henry suggested that the reason for our 'affinity' is that we are both beautiful Nubian creatures. I wanted to vomit, but the whisky held me down. Drink is good for drowning out nausea; I swear by it.

It is quiet here in the country. I can hear birdsong. I can hear the sound of a helicopter overhead.

I take a right

towards the town centre and then

I am walking by a stream in the park and thinking about love/money.

My phone is ringing and it is Henry but I let it ring off. I am in a mess, to tell you the truth. The red letters are mounting up. I have more than four substantial bills, plus there is the rent due on my room. I need to make a lot of money in the next three days

Henry is phoning again, apologizing for this morning, over and over. I tell him that I'm having a problem with some bills. There is a silence and he asks me to come back. Says that we can talk about it.

Back at the house, Henry wants to know if I want to lie down upstairs for a while.

I see that he has put aside another envelope for me by the stove in the kitchen, which makes up the rent for this month. Just.

I slept badly last night and am not in the mood to pretend I am enjoying something that I'm not.

I think that the dismay is showing on my face, so he asks me if I want something strong to drink.

There is only ever one answer to that.

We sit in his drawing room and drink whisky and sing songs and then we go up to bed. The whisky takes effect on Henry who, thank God, falls asleep and then I do.

An hour or so later he is lying behind me whispering my name again and again. You make me like this, he says. You must excuse me. I feel so sexual when I'm with you. You just bring something out in me.

I count to ten.

1 Henry has stopped whispering my name
2 because he has fallen out of the bed
3 and is sprawled out on the floor,
4 giggling, completely drunk. I
5 climb out of the bed and he is
6 lying on his back, helpless and naked.
7 Giggling just like a baby.
8 This is sick
9 I do not know whether to laugh or cry.
10 This is fucked.

Without thinking too much, I begin to put on my clothes for the second time today. I leave the knickers on the carpet by his head. He doesn't seem to know quite what is going on.

He is saying my name again and watching me put on my clothes, trying to compute

drunk and trying to compute.

I leave the room.

I walk down the stairs and he is still calling my name.

He has daughters. He has a family. It does not seem fair that someone so old should have a doting family and someone as young as me should have no one.

I can hear Henry's voice coming from upstairs. He sounds a bit desperate now. As though he's panicking a bit. I'm in the kitchen. I call 999 on the phone.

a) 'I was walking by this old man's house.' I say
or
b) 'I'm a nurse. He's taken a bit of a fall.'
or
c) 'I'm a friend of the neighbour and I saw the door open, so, naturally, I rushed in to investigate.'

I give them the address.

I hang up.

The cream envelope is over on the worktop, by the side door. From his basket, Davies gives me a long look.

I open the latch on the back door. Davies is at my feet. Taking a deep breath, I feel awake. I breeze out of the house and up the stony path. Davies is running with me. Outside the sky is pink and I don't feel bad,

not even a bit.

11 I hear sirens.

I wonder how he was, my father. Tall. Blackshining I
wonder who he was. If I knew that, then perhaps I could
understand what is happening.

Half inside a dream and a half inside something else,
a man appears out of the dark light of the morning, his back
to me. I reach out my hands. He could be my father, this man.
His neck is the same colour. His hair, soft, silver-black. He turns
around

and the homeless man asks me for money.

I give my father fifteen hard-earned pounds and stagger
home, my hands on my face. I remember who I am, I think.

An African,

one most magical African
on a bridge on Primrose Hill. I shudder.

I am three sheets to the wind, perhaps. This earth tunnel.
This life thing, it's frightening.

What are the codes to the thing? I thought I had them once,
armed with my great knowledge of the Bible, and the blue
powder dream-book, which disappeared when Mum did.

What is the code to feeling exactly like you belong?

I stagger over Primrose Hill Bridge. It is November and
already bitterly cold. I keep my head down, quite invisible in
this picture-book scene, especially in the twilight. I search
hard in the cracks on the ground to see Signs, Facts and Other
Things, pining for the sight of my brother. I wonder,

is he still a seer of things?

Will I burn in hell perhaps

and if I am resigned to that fact, where
is the way out? Will dying hurt at all?

Could it hurt more than life, in any case? What is the code
to being able to see straight? On what timeline is the lady
passing me in the street with her yoga mat while I stumble
around the dark? Are timelines measured by number, and if so,
what are the winning coordinates? Is life an illusion too? Is it
liquid silver, like Time?

One day Little Roo and I were digging for treasure in my
auntie's garden and Grandma came out and said, you dig and
you dig, *child*, and you'll get to Australia.

So where is our Australia? We've been digging,
it seems, for years. Is life hidden in the lining of our seams?
Are we wearing it inside out?

data

I think William really loved you, said Grandma.
Let me tell you the story.

One day, the sun was shining, she said,
and William appeared at the front door. He had dirt on his
boots. I saw from the upstairs window
him changing them in the car, getting all fresh for us,
putting on some lovely brown shoes.
That's him, I said. That's him all over.
Grandma nodded.
That boy really loved you
he came straight up.
He looked me in the eye and said
I love your granddaughter, so so much
and I want to marry her. I promise,
I promise to take care of her.
And Granddad nodded and said that was fine by him.
She paused. Patted her head wrap.
What's he doing now? These days?
I think he has a girl,
I said
Some girl. I don't know who.
I caught myself screwing my face up.
Poor girl, said Grandma. He really loves you. He'll always
love you.
But William was much like a lot of things. So good he didn't
seem real enough.

I nod and I nod but I don't tell Grandma

he called me every other day for the first three years. He
remembered every birthday. He was always, always there.

I don't say,

now if I call him, the line goes dead.

My mother's formidable north star is still busying herself in
the kitchen.

Yes, he loves me, I say.

Shame it didn't work out.

Granddad hobbles out of the living room, on the way
upstairs. It takes him a great amount of time to move around
these days. Granddad is different. Softer and quite unsure of
the world.

He smiles, eyes crinkling

and says,

'I was going to tell you you look like Yrsa. You look a lot like
Yrsa.'

the animals

Fredrick Stimpson still doesn't know what you look like. Answers the door blindfolded. Likes to pretend he's a household pet. Likes being made to fetch things and wash your worn underwear with his hands. (Remembering not to wash your underwear is harder than it sounds.) Fredrick Stimpson is painfully shy, so he stays fully clothed the whole time. His house is a large, large one

(all these grown men in houses that swallow them). You talk about the rain. He sounds like he's from further south. He grew up on a farm, and it shows.

The first time he shows you how to handle him, you are mesmerized.

You take to it easily though. What a wondrous exchange. Ever heard a cane whip through the air? Slicing atoms. Whoosh. Crack.

Fredrick Stimpson always has the money. And that's why you see him, of course. Let's be honest.

Fredrick Stimpson

is partial to being chastised

wonders if he's done something wrong

on the weeks you go under

and he doesn't hear from you. He calls you mistress on the phone,

says

your pet misses you.

OLD-FASHIONED HAMPSTEAD HOME. YOU
and MALCOLM *are sitting in his blue Victorian-style*
living room.

MALCOLM
It's like we don't get a summertime at all, in this country.

YOU
Not at all. Terrible.

MALCOLM
Green tea or peppermint?

YOU
Oh, peppermint. You know me. Haha.

MALCOLM
Oh, of course, I remember – you don't like green tea.

YOU
Gives me stomach ache.

MALCOLM
Ah yes, stomach ache.

> *Silence. You both stare at the TV.* MALCOLM *is always*
> *nervous to begin with.* YOU *stare at the television. Beads of*
> *sweat are forming on his forehead.* MALCOLM *is a lover*
> *of china dolls. They adorn his bookshelves and cabinets.*

MALCOLM

I lost some weight last week.

YOU

Oh, wow, well done.

MALCOLM

Yes, thank you. I suppose the trick is to make sure it stays off. Not so good at that. *[Hangs his head shamefully]* I'm an over-Indulger.

YOU

[Needing this to be hurried along]
And might you need to be punished?

MALCOLM

Oh, of course . . . the notes! I'm always forgetting to email!

MALCOLM *hands* YOU *the notes and hangs nervously by the piano as you read.*

YOU

Ah. Headmistress. Headmistress today.

MALCOLM

[Clears throat] You're a fast reader! Haha.
[Now unsure] Um. Is that okay?

YOU

Oh, Yeah, sure. I just need to

[YOU *open your coat and you're wearing the Wrong Thing – the leather all-in-one.*]
. . . change.

MALCOLM
Oh, I am sorry, I should have said. I'm sorry. I am sorry.

YOU
No, no worries at all, it's quite alright. May I use your bathroom? I'll be two minutes.

MALCOLM
But of course.

YOU *go to the bathroom and struggle to peel this leather costume off your skin. It takes longer than expected. Your silk blouse is creased, but thank God you brought it. YOU change into a tweed pencil skirt and put the shoes back on. MALCOLM calls to you from the hallway . . .*

MALCOLM
Ready!

YOU
Righty ho.

INTERIOR:
STUDY.

MALCOLM's *paddles, switches and two canes are arranged neatly on the polished walnut desk. The money has been placed diligently in a brown envelope.* YOU *pop it into your handbag.* YOU *study yourself in the mirror. You're an actress, and you're wonderful.*

MALCOLM *appears, sheepishly, in a school uniform. On first glance it is ridiculous. But we all have needs and you have a heart. Making people feel good must be taken seriously.*

YOU
Get out again and knock.

MALCOLM *disappears at once. A timid knock follows.*

YOU
Yes?

MALCOLM *walks into view, his head low*

skin flushed.

YOU
Come here,
boy.

son.

Sonny goes and dies quietly.
Like a punk, says Roo.
Can you believe he died
says Roo. *That mother fucker. He was ill, I heard. Was working*
myself up to maybe visiting him in hospital, I don't know. To talk
everything out, really try with him. To be a son. Or at least an
acquaintance. Ha. Isn't that a shitter
growls Roo into the headset
He wasn't worth it. I say.
Are you okay? I say
Got a cold, he says,

        and I think about these parents of ours
                  our makers
      our stars. (Such impossible, complex stars.)
            How they came, exploded,
                and fell away.

They are not ours, the stars,
and never have been.

Be mindful.

horrible info

Something is stopping you from getting out of bed.
Fact. Things are as grey as you can possibly imagine Fact.
You're falling under.
Fact. You are no one's child anymore
and your hands are still cold. You drink red wine to soften
the edges of the day. But there are bad things curling the
edges, brown/
black . . . and the wine is giving you headaches. Fact.
Migraines. Fact./
The terrible is in your throat
the dark does not know how to get out of you
the darkness burns a hole in your liver;
it is too much
and it is not enough
it is almost unbearable.
Drink vodka and red wine at the weekends
make countless new friends at night
delete their numbers during the week
because names, you can hardly remember names.
You must go somewhere else. There is not enough light.
Some days you can't breathe: you know what that feels like;
when you are bored at night
and everything bad is
loud and important.
Take to the streets, It's a one-time thing, this life
You've got to move. When in doubt, always move.
Or you ain't going to make it.

green:
a run

Someone says one day
above the din. Above the constant fever.
'You'd make a lot of money in South Africa, you know. All
the models there look similar to you. I reckon you could do it.'
You don't need to hear anything else. You set off. Cape Town
bound
    with one hundred and eighty pounds in your bag.

Roo calls.

What is it, you say
I'm literally on a plane. I'm going to South Africa

Where? How come?

South Africa. I have to.
I have to go
away.
I haven't been feeling very well
not very well at all.
(You want to cry, but don't.)

Raa, says Roo.

I promise to call, you say. When I'm settled.

One thing I have to tell you first,
says your brother.
but he doesn't speak
he really doesn't.

They are telling us to switch off our phones
What?
Hurry up, man,
you say
the woman's going to shout at me
You hear him breathing.
It's reassuring, hearing the air of those you love the most.

Today I met my daughter.

What? You say
Yeah.
says Roo
I didn't know either. I feel amazing;
there's nothing like it.
I held her and it was everything.

Oh my God

You say.
Oh my God
you say.
Oh my God, you have a daughter!
You say
I'm so happy for you. For us.

And the lady is coming over to tell you to please hang up the
phone and you say
Roo.
Roo.
We're literally taking off.
I have to go
I have to go
but I LOVE YOU
and her
and I'll call you when I land.

Listen to you, he says
Raa.
Listen to you getting all emotional.
Shut up, you say, and hang up.

awayness; an almanac

You may not run away from the thing that you are
because it comes and comes and comes as sure as you
breathe. As certain. The thing is deep inside your linings, way
down in the marrow. People have a lot of words for it.

There are ten thousand names for it and you. Wherever you
are, it catches you up. It catches you in South Africa. Wherever
you are and whatever it is, the terrible is trying to grip you and
sometimes you're walking down the street and it tries to knock
you clean off your feet and send you right underground. The
terrible comes like a bang in the night. It takes a drink and
several more and comes to plague you in the morning; it damn
near poisons you with all the drink it needs to stay alive. It toys
with you the morning after – stays the entire day, squeezing
you by the shoulders, making your hands shake. It smiles at
you, the terrible. Sitting, arms folded, in the corner of the
room. It just can't help itself. It just needs friends.

It's such a lonely thing.

The terrible needs to eat and it eats whole lives up in one
sitting.

The terrible claps its terrible hands and everything falls right
through them. The terrible is here one month and gone for a
while until the middle of the next, allowing you to catch your
breath – and just when you almost think everything is okay
and when you are not over- or under-breathing, it surprises you
in the middle of the night again. You find another kind doctor,
with long hair. According to him, the terrible needs to drink
more water – to take more walks, the terrible needs vitamin D
and does not need anti-anxiety medicine; perhaps a dose of

CBT on account of the OCD. On account of the mild germ phobia.

The terrible breathes a sigh of relief. It will not take pills because it doesn't believe in them but it does believe in spirulina, becomes vegan, becomes gluten free, takes some long walks in the sun

detoxes, removes the heavy metal from its terrible system. It wants to stop drinking but can't, wants to call Roo but never, ever does. The terrible screams at your mother in amber nightmares and cannot understand for the life of it why you don't want to take it to bed with you. It climbs in with you anyway; and it's just as you thought. The terrible wakes up shuddering and BELLOWS

and you try to lock it out of your room but it seeps under the gap between the door and the floor.

The terrible meets a strange man in a bar who tells you that black people in his country are lazy and the terrible jumped right out and almost stabbed him

the terrible shocks you in ways that you could never imagine,

tripping you up, doing things you shouldn't do and things that you wouldn't do

making a fool of you. It is shifty, and sometimes invisible, or on holiday. A good decision here, some abstinence there, some moderation there and you'll think it's left you alone but then you're walking and the terrible is a hole waiting to catch you. A fucking hole in the ground. The terrible is why you cannot call your grandparents and the terrible is why no one can hear from Roo and the terrible is no Roo and distance from Samson and the reason why, when Grandma takes Marcia's ashes away from the house, nobody complains. The terrible is a wall of smoke, always getting in the way, obscuring everything. William calls on your birthday, this year and the next and the next and the terrible will not return his calls

making you wonder what kind of godless spirit destroys a
perfectly beautiful thing. It trips you up to trip you up to trip
you. It gathers around your neck like a charm, a teardrop of
rust. It puts a hole in your throat and stuffs it up with
    yarn.
The terrible sighs (again).
The terrible gets warm inside when the man that is trouble
buys you one last whisky, the one to take you over the edge
The terrible cries and cannot believe it when you're picked
for the job over the other girls; its flips turn your belly upside
down; the terrible takes you out for ice cream and no dinner
when you sell Marcia's house after Two and a Half DAMN
YEARS and starves itself of alcohol. Perhaps it is your friend.
Perhaps the terrible is your heart. Perhaps the terrible loves
you, after all?
    Don't you know I've been carrying you throughout all this?
    says the terrible
Don't you know you're one of the lucky ones? shouts the
terrible. Don't you know I've got you, you ungrateful,
ungrateful creature? You wretch! Don't you know those dark
times kept you stronger? (thus sayeth the terrible) Don't you
know without me you would be just another girl with an
everyday life and an almost-house always under construction
and a man you tolerate and don't really love and a father you
met but who stopped you from doing anything and seeing the
world, don't you know you'd be a boring woman with bills
and a horrible job and wrinkles around her eyes and babies
and babies and a mortgage and savings and boring sex or no
sex and a lukewarm life, DON'T YOU KNOW I
FUCKING KEPT YOU SAFE??? bellows the terrible, its
yellow eyes gleaming. Don't you know I gave you the best
timelines, a glittering story, a punchline, a reason to live, don't
you know the drugs didn't kill you – they could have or should

have and never did – don't you know your life has been one magic spell cast after the other, are you stupid, screams the terrible . . . well, are you? Don't you know that without me you diediedie in the mundane? Have you learned nothing? Don't you know you earned resilience? Don't you know I KEPT YOU RICH!!! No . . . I didn't think so, sniffed

the terrible, shaking his.her.their head(s) violently in the wind,

turning away from each other and the world,

and why did you never love me?

demands the terrible

her.his.their glittering yellow eyes wet with rage.

The terrible has always been there for you. It's true. At least since books and Mum and the worktop. It appears to you in many forms. In the night, you are arguing with Marcia, who becomes Linford. David is knocking at your door, grinning the grin of death. The lightswitches won't work. There is a cat on the ceiling. Your grandparents wear glittery wings and fly into your room late at night. You answer a knock on the door and the cat walks in, seething, just like he owns the place. There is a lion in your bed. There are scratches on the kitchen floor. Mum camps out in your dreams, your father appears, his back to you, and when he turns around he is Scott Bakula. You can't sleep at night. What are the codes for the good and happy things?

Did you drown?

What are the coordinates to a place above sea level?

No one can tread water forever. No one can swallow salt and brine and bile forever. And if we are to survive, what's it for what is it all for and why why why all the pain why natural disaster why politics why war why danger every single day why the everlasting blanket of short breath and stress, anxiety and panic, why the frequency of fear are we coming of age till we die might we burn up in hellfire because we are wrong things always wrong things doing the wrong things why does the world hate black people is this a world is this the only world is it true, all of it, the Bible? Is there God is there a God and is God for us or against us? Did we displease the Holy Trinity might we die will we die will we live will any of us live and make it into the eternal life afterwards is the earth ruined for good. Is it global warming why is the climate shifting. What turns a milk sky pink? Is it the sins of the world, bleeding up into the atmopshere reddening the clouds up above or is it love. Could it be love? Jesus Christ,

can there be love?

There will be more love.

says the sky

There will be more love.

[i]

a girl walks into the bar and
you are the girl. You and the terrible are drinking alone,
sitting close to each other, holding hands, cosying up like old
sweethearts. The barman says to you
'why the long face?'
When he asks you your name, you are not sure the words come
out.

(ii)

a girl in a bar tosses her hair, drinks the second whisky
and feels better, teetering on the bar. The girl says waass-all-
thisss then?
The barman says
a night where people talk
They talk?
They talk, he says. Mostly in poetry
he says.
You like poetry? You remember poetry?
There is something underneath your seams; you remember
poetry. They say write your thoughts out. So you do, and you do
and you do. They say write a poem about discord in the family,
if you can. Next Monday, if you can.
Come read it,
If you can.
You laugh. You say, Yeah. Yeah I think I could do that.

The terrible writes poetry, impresses people
The terrible writes poetry impresses people
                              and the terrible writes poetry
impresses people
    after all, it takes six moments to write a thing
1 you dream

                              2 you wake up

3 you sit down

                              4 you settle on the chair/bed/floor

5 you think what is
happening? is this the day
when nothing'll come? is
this the end of it?

                              6 then you grip
                              your heart, involuntarily
                              and your soul comes up. Your
                              soul comes up, I'm telling you.

No such thing as a block, not really.
    Your soul arises and you let it; or you don't.

Epilogue

The Time is now.

Roo and I are parked up in the car. We were on the way to pick up the kids from their mother's. He has three children now. I am back up North for the weekend to see our grandparents because Grandma is turning ninety.

The sky has faded somewhat in the north of England. I'm sure there was more colour back when we were kids, but that can't be true. Unless the world is slowly paling.

It is early morning time. We're parked right opposite the house to see what we can see. We arrived with enough time to take a smart detour and stake out our old place. Clean, functional people live there now – you can tell by the paint job on the porch and the ordered lawn. There is a new high wooden gate out back, so we can't quite see everything. There is one of those mobile homes parked outside, though, so I assume that the garden is kept well these days.

'Looks like the best people got the job,' Roo says, wincing.

They kept the rosebush, though, and the conservatory. The small potted plant in the front is a shapely fern now. The house still whispers *Marcia*'s. The cemetery is small and quiet, much more beautiful than I remember.

The hallway light is on inside. I want to ring the doorbell. Ask if I can look around inside, but I daren't. It could be too different in there;

or worse, the same.

The moon is in the morning sky, round and obstinate as it ever was. We giggle, because Roo has turned on the local radio and here comes the DJ talking in that broad Chorley accent.

Bitty McLean's version of 'Dedicated to the One I Love' starts playing

and this song always reminds me of Marcia Daley-Ward. God, could she dance.

An old lady comes around the corner. Her hair and face are white and she has a neon-green walking stick. She catches my eye and stands still for a moment. Deliberately, she begins to cross into the space where we are parked. People are nosy round these parts. This was our neighbourhood, though. We have as much right to be here as anyone else.

She looks to be coming over to us.

When at last she gets to the car I wind down my window, ready for whatever she has to say. She shifts on her walking stick and takes a breath before speaking, her eyes moving beween Roo and me.

'Hello, how are you?'

'Um . . . good,' I say. 'And you?'

'You lived here once, didn't you?'

Surprised, I nod.

'I remember you both,' she says. 'Didn't you live here with your mother?'

This stops me for a moment. I clear my throat. I say,

'We did, but it's been a while. Both moved away now. I haven't been back for seven, eight years.'

'Ten,' says Roo. 'Nearly ten.'

'Yes,' she says. 'Yes. I remember you both.'

I don't remember her at all. Roo is quite silent.

'Round the back of you, I lived,' she continues, as though reading our thoughts.

'My husband died four years ago, of course, and your neighbours that were here, on this side are gone too.

Really special children you were. We always used to think that.'

and then,

'Will you be staying long? Won't you come and visit?'

No one says anything.

'I reckon it's going to rain,' she says.

Roo nods and I look at the sky.

'I have to get back to London,' I say. 'But another time.'

'Yeah,' says Roo. 'Sometime soon.'

'Well, good luck, you two, good luck,' she says. 'I'm going to try and catch this bus now.'

I say thank you, and smile and nod, and wind up the window. Roo falls silent again.

Bitty Mclean sings on:

'Each night before you go to bed my baby
Whisper a little prayer for me my baby'

and I lean my head back on the headrest, remembering my hands in Marcia's. How she could move like no one else.

There is a low rumble in the sky.

All of a sudden, my brother's eyes appear to dart beyond the passenger window. He moves suddenly

and accidentally drops his cigarette out of the window.

'What???' I say, 'Look at the rosebush,'
'what's up?' says Roo.

'Whaaat? 'I swear something just
What you talking about?' moved. Raa! That's a mad
ting.'

'Get lost.' But Roo's face hasn't
changed.
It's no joke, it seems. No
joke at all.

I look where he's looking
and I see the thing too.

What luck. What terrific magic.

YRSA DALEY-WARD

'You will come away bruised.
You will come away bruised
but this will give you poetry.'

Raw and stark, the poems in Yrsa Daley-Ward's
breakthrough collection strip down her
reflections on the heart, life, the inner self,
coming of age, faith and loss to their essence.
They resonate to the core of experience.

**'yrsa daley-ward's 'bone' is a symphony of
breaking and mending. an expert storyteller.
of the rarest. and purest kind — daley-ward
is uncannily attentive and in tune to the
things beneath life. beneath the skin.
beneath the weather of the everyday.'**

Nayyirah Waheed, author of *salt.* and *nejma.*

'One of the must-reads of the year'

Rohan Silva, *Evening Standard*

WWW.PENGUIN.CO.UK